By the 1940s the Gators' football stadium, Florida Field, stood in the midst of athletic facilities that included a baseball field, tennis courts, and a track—all of which allowed students and faculty to spend much of their free time outdoors, exercising and witnessing sporting events in comfort.

HISTORIC PHOTOS OF
UNIVERSITY OF
FLORIDA FOOTBALL

TEXT AND CAPTIONS BY KEVIN MCCARTHY

TURNER
PUBLISHING COMPANY

HISTORIC PHOTOS OF
UNIVERSITY OF
FLORIDA FOOTBALL

Turner Publishing Company
www.turnerpublishing.com

Historic Photos of University of Florida Football

Copyright © 2009 Turner Publishing Company

Library of Congress Control Number: 2008908519

ISBN-13: 978-1-59652-514-6

Printed in the United States of America

ISBN 978-1-68442-080-3 (hc)

CONTENTS

The first unofficial coach of the football team when the school was in Lake City, Florida, was Professor James Farr (second from left, bottom row, in this 1911 photograph). Farr was also the head of the English Department. The president of the school during the 1901–1902 school term, Dr. T. H. Taliaferro, offered to help Farr in coaching the team if time would allow.

Acknowledgments

This volume, *Historic Photos of University of Florida Football*, was possible only through the cooperation of University of Florida archivists Carl Van Ness and Joyce Dewsbury. The archives at the Florida Department of State in Tallahassee were also invaluable in the search for old photographs. It is with great thanks and appreciation that we acknowledge the valuable contributions of officials at both institutions for their generous support. The photographs within this volume were chosen from the collections at the University of Florida and at the Florida Department of State and are used by permission.

PREFACE

Football success would have been hard to predict for the University of Florida in its early years. Especially after its 1904 team in Lake City was outscored 224–0. Once the school moved to its present location in Gainesville, Florida, it began to do better and then still better, beating a school like Florida Southern 144–0 and holding its own against Southern powerhouses Alabama, Georgia, and Georgia Tech. Like that of many schools, the progress has been slow and often plagued by setbacks, but—with a commitment to excellence in all fields, both academic and athletic—that progress has culminated in a consistently winning program.

The photographs on the following pages trace the history of football at what is today one of the true bastions of gridiron superiority. They point out how UF has won three national championships in the last three decades, has produced three Heisman Trophy winners, and has sent forth hundreds of ballplayers to excel in the National Football League and, even more important, in the fields of business, education, law, medicine, religion, and service.

These images have been selected from archives in Gainesville and Tallahassee and have been captioned with short explanations describing the scenes depicted. With the exception of touching up imperfections that have accrued with the passage of time and cropping where necessary, no changes have been made. The focus and clarity of many images are limited by the technology and the ability of the photographer at the time they were taken. In many cases, the photos have not been seen by the public for decades, if ever. Now with the Gator Nation exceeding 250,000 living alumni and with the student body more than 50,000, interest in all things associated with the University of Florida is high.

While many people around the nation and world associate the University of Florida with the Fightin' Gators, it is my fondest hope that interest in the football program will extend to interest in the school's many academic accomplishments. And that pride in being associated with the school will lead to even more highly qualified students studying there, adding to the number of alumni and friends supporting the institution's many efforts to make this world a better place to live.

As the state's oldest, largest, and most comprehensive university, the University of Florida is the nation's fourth-largest. Its more than 50,000 students study in ideal surroundings of more than 2,000 acres in a city that prides itself on beauty and culture. The athletic teams in general, and the football program in particular, have done much to put UF on the sports map. In fact, only UF and UCLA appear in the top ten in each of the last 25 national all-sports rankings. More important, UF's 89 percent graduation rate among athletes in recent years has made clear to students and alumni alike how important the college diploma is. The high demands that the more than 4,000 faculty place on the students, including the athletes, ensure that a UF degree is a valuable commodity in preparing them for the post-school world.

Here then is the story of the many successes and some failures of the storied UF football program, how the tears of desperation in the early years have consistently given way to the euphoria associated with high rankings and victories.

—*Kevin McCarthy*

The simple sign on the corner of University Avenue and 13th Street after the school opened in Gainesville in 1906 would become more elaborate as student numbers increased. By 2006 the university had more than 50,000 students, many of whom would be part of the 90,000 and more fans attending a home game each fall. The school has been one of the strongest economic forces in Alachua County since the early 1900s.

Early Roads to Gridiron Greatness

(1853–1929)

The University of Florida traces its beginnings to 1851, when the Seminary Act of 1851 established two seminaries for the newly established state. Where exactly those two schools, one east of the Suwannee River and one west of that river, would be was to be determined by which towns were willing to help fund them. The East Florida Independent Institute, which had opened in Ocala south of Gainesville in 1852, became the East Florida Seminary in 1853, whereas Tallahassee became the site of the second seminary, the one that would become the Florida State College and—much later—Florida State University.

The East Florida Seminary struggled until 1861, when it closed at the outbreak of the Civil War. The school reopened in Gainesville after the war and allowed students as young as twelve or thirteen to enroll. Both boys and girls attended the school. According to school regulations, students were not allowed to drink liquor, smoke, or enter a billiards room, saloon, or "house of ill-fame."

Meanwhile the Florida Agricultural College opened in 1884 in the town of Lake City about 40 miles north of Gainesville. At first only men were allowed to attend the school, the first in Florida to call itself a college. Women began attending in 1894. Officials changed the name of the school to the University of Florida in 1903. In the following year the University of Florida Athletic Association was founded, and several football games were played (and lost), but UF's official media guide does not include those games. The East Florida Seminary and the Florida Agricultural College were both antecedents of UF.

The school was moved to Gainesville after passage of the Buckman Act of 1905, much to the displeasure of the local people in Lake City, and classes opened up at the new campus in 1906. Women were not allowed to take classes there during the regular academic year, but instead were to study at the State College for Women in Tallahassee. UF prospered and grew each year as it attracted more and more students and built up the campus. By 1927, the Florida land boom burst, and the fortunes of the state began to decline. It would take a decade for the university to get back on its feet.

The town of Gainesville, which had been established in 1854, was incorporated in 1869, four years after the Civil War ended. By 1884, when this sketch was made, the town had about 2,000 residents, along with fourteen cotton gins, three railroads, and many citrus and vegetable farms. What it did not have was a college or university. Those interested in a higher education looked to Lake City to the north, which did.

The immediate predecessor of the University of Florida in Gainesville was Florida Agricultural College (FAC) in Lake City to the north. Established in 1884, the school was located in Lake City partly because of the town's excellent climate, and partly, in the words of education officials, because of the community's "high reputation for morality and love of order."

Another predecessor of UF and of the Gator football team was the team fielded by East Florida Seminary (EFS) in Gainesville, shown here in 1902. The school opened in 1854 in Ocala, but moved north to Gainesville in 1866, after the Civil War. The school had 71 students in 1866 and 225 in 1904. The football team played other Florida schools.

A very early football team at the Florida Agricultural College was the 1902 team shown here. Official records of the Gator football team don't begin until the school reopened in Gainesville (1906), but the FAC team played (and lost) a game to Stetson University in 1901, presumably because a stump in the middle of the field prevented the Gators from scoring. FAC also lost a game in 1902 to Stetson, 6–5.

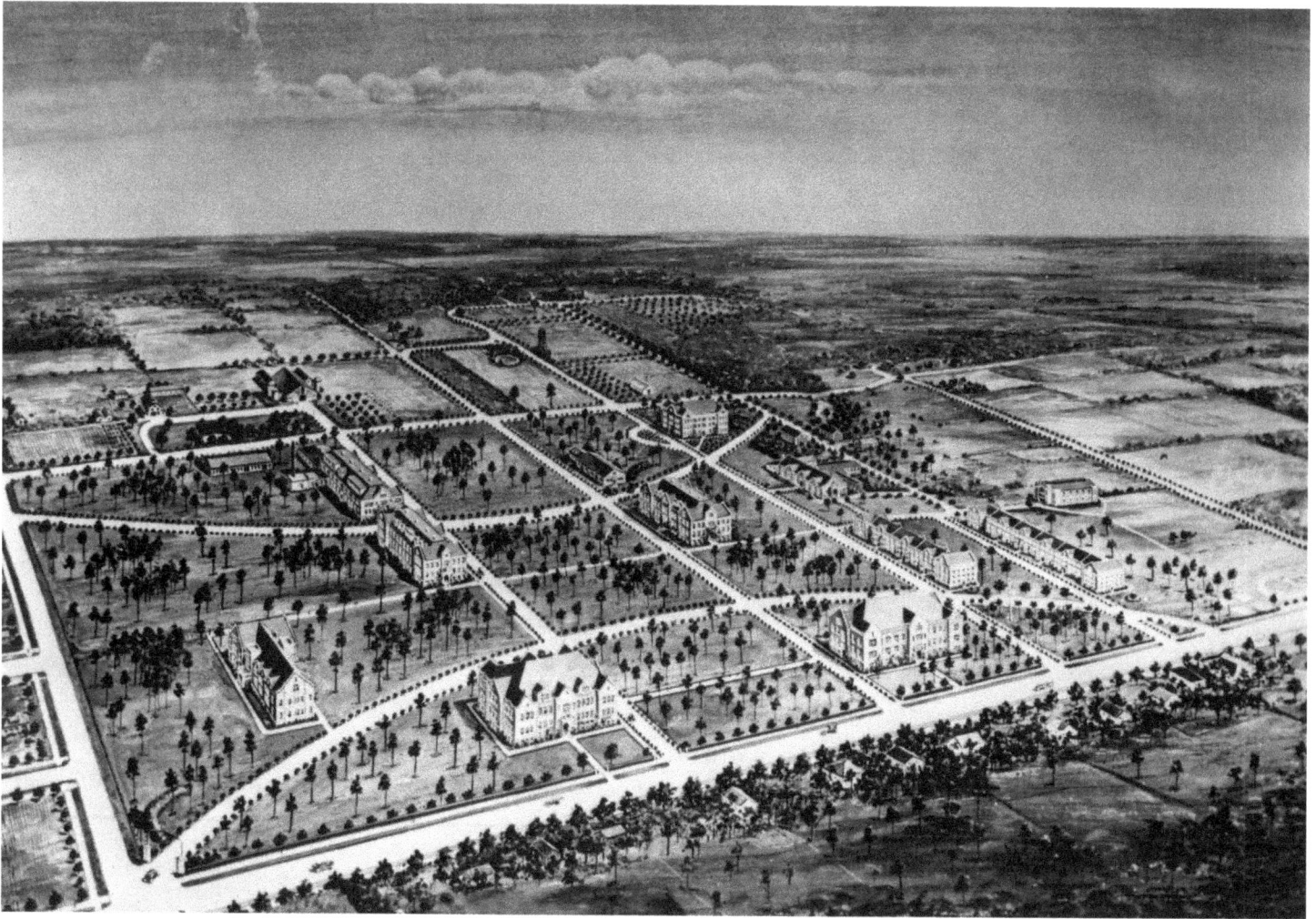

A sketch of the planned campus of the University of Florida in Gainesville shows wide, open spaces on a large tract of land. The center of town was at the intersection of what would become Main Street and University Avenue, about a mile east of the campus. The initial enrollment in 1906 was about 100 students, including 38 "sub-freshmen," students taking courses in order to gain admission to the school.

An early UF team was the 1907 squad, which held an excellent 4-0-1 record. Coach James Forsythe sits in the middle row, second from left. Starring on that team was William "Willie" Shands (bottom row, far right), who later became a state senator and the one most responsible for having the state's medical school established at UF in 1958. Shands Hospital is named in his honor.

Roy Corbett, captain of the 1907 Gator team. He claimed that he was the first student to register at the new University of Florida when it opened for classes in Gainesville in 1906. Players on those early teams were given a jersey and pants, but had to provide their own shoes, headgear (if they chose to wear it), and all protective clothing.

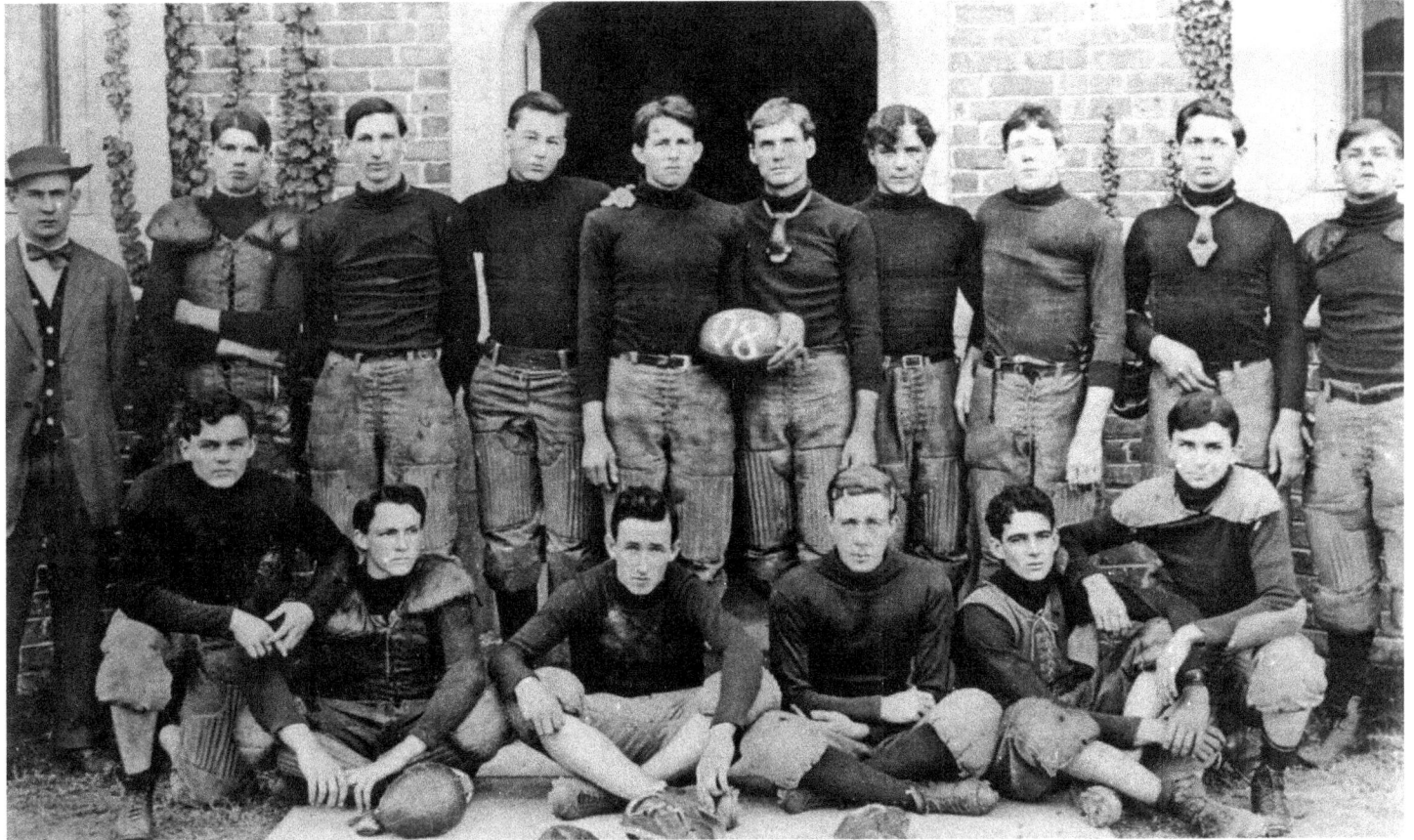

Some of the players on the 1908 team wear nose guards around their necks for the official group shot. Equipment was sparse in those days, and some players refused to wear the helmets, which—though made only of leather—added some protection for their heads. The coach in those early games was James "Pee Wee" Forsythe, who coached for three seasons (1906–1908), enjoying a 14-6-2 record.

In a 1908 game against Jacksonville's Riverside Athletic Club in south Jacksonville, the Gators won 4–0 at a time when both touchdowns and field goals counted for 4 points. Spectators in their finest outfits stand along the sidelines, long before stadium seating with skyboxes and replay screens. The Gators beat the Athletic Club in each of the six matches they played against each other.

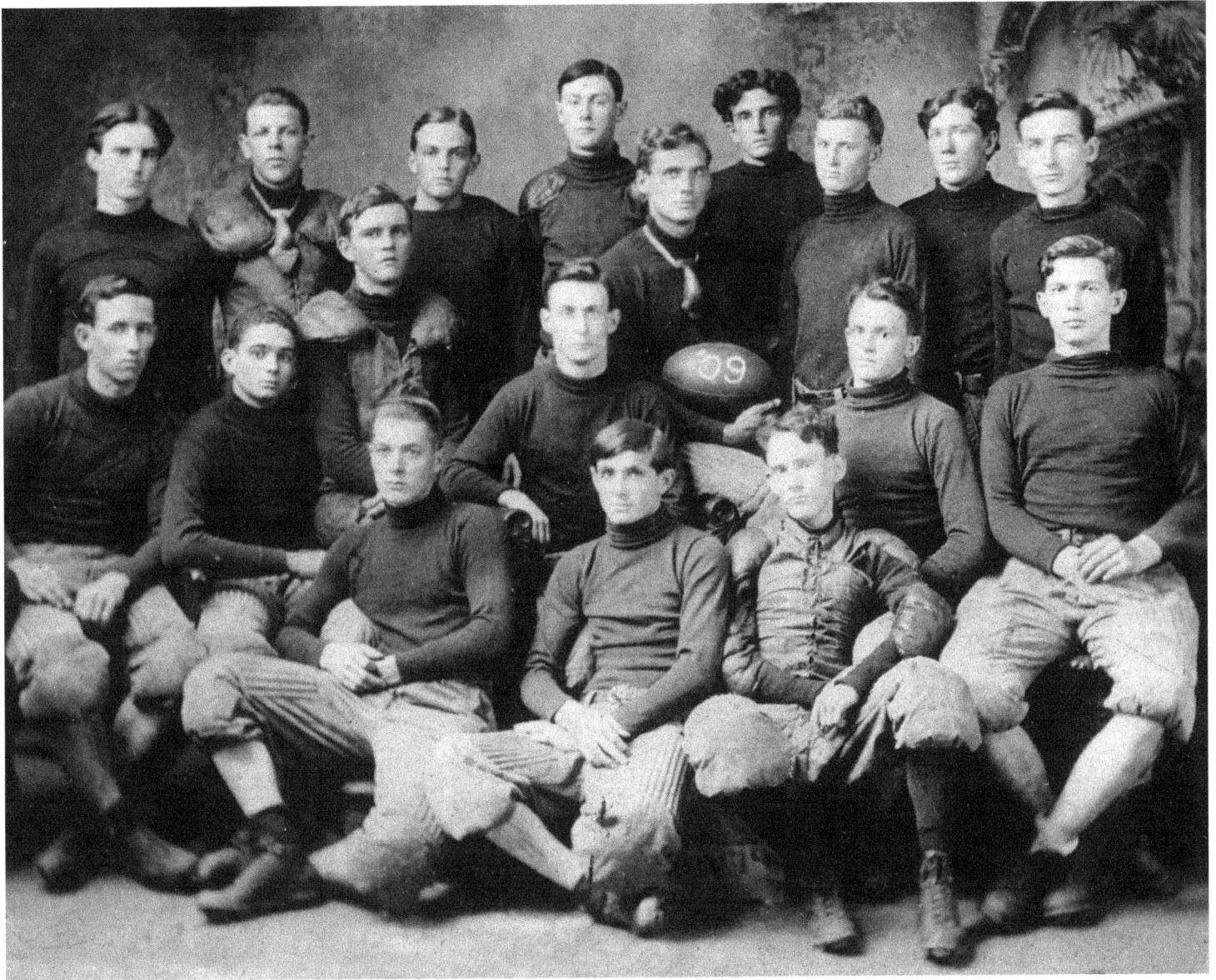

In the 1909 team photograph, the person sitting on the first row, fifth from left, is Coach G. E. Pyle, who coached the team from 1909 to 1913, built a record of 26-7-3, and increased the competition from local teams and two state colleges, Rollins and Stetson, by joining the Southern Intercollegiate Athletic Association. His 1913 team beat Florida Southern by the largest margin of any Gator football game: 144–0.

Early team photos included a football with the date of that season painted on it, making it easy for future editors. Coach Pyle's 1910 team became UF's highest-scoring one up to that time, racking up 186 points and allowing only 15. The team poses with President Albert A. Murphree (in the back, at left), the second head of the school after the move to Gainesville from Lake City.

The 1912 team also posed with President Murphree. As president from 1909 to 1927, a crucial time in the history of the young school, Murphree did much to put UF on the road to excellence in many fields. Of American football, he noted that the sport "develops intuition, cultivates mental alertness, self-control, and physical manhood."

In 1912, education officials awarded a contract for the construction of Floyd Hall, a three-story building that would house the College of Agriculture, in which the building's namesake, Major Wilbur Floyd, was assistant dean (1915–1938). During the 1918 Spanish influenza epidemic that swept the country and the UF campus, Floyd Hall was converted into a temporary hospital. The building was restored in 1992 and renamed Griffin-Floyd Hall.

The man for whom UF's athletic dorm, Yon Hall, is named, Everett Yon, poses in this 1915 varsity photo, fourth from the left, at rear. In the mid-1920s, he would work as an assistant coach under James Van Fleet. The 1915 team held a poor 4-3 record and the distinction of being shut out by Auburn, Sewanee, and Georgia, but shutting out Florida Southern and the Citadel.

In the 1900–1919 era, fans could stand on the sidelines or drive their cars up to the field and watch from the comfort of their vehicles, standing on the front seat for an even better view. Facilities remained limited until the 1930s, when UF built a large stadium for spectators, a facility that increased in size as the team prospered.

The freshmen football players at UF, who were not allowed to compete against the varsity, played their own schedule against out-of-town opponents. In the 1920s, they did so well one season, going undefeated, that the UF yearbook labeled them "Champions of the South."

En route to playing and losing to Harvard, 24–0, in Massachusetts, the 1922 Gator team stopped off in Washington, D.C., where they toured the city and Capitol and then visited the White House. Shown here at the White House, the players and coaches shook hands with President Warren Harding, whom they cheered loudly since it was his birthday.

The 1923 Florida football team, shown here, was at the forefront of two longtime rivalries that would continue to the present: the Georgia Bulldogs, a rivalry that began in 1915, and the Kentucky Wildcats, a rivalry that began in 1917. The Wildcats excelled in basketball; the Bulldogs offered a tougher test on the gridiron.

Early Gator home games, like this one between the Gators and Mercer College, were played on Fleming Field, which is today between West University Avenue and the stadium. The baseball team also used Fleming Field, as did professional baseball teams like the Boston Red Sox and New York Giants. The Gators played Mercer 17 times between 1906 and 1928 and racked up a 10-6-1 record against them.

Captain James Van Fleet, a West Point graduate, coached the 1923 Gators, nicknamed "the team that fought the Army." Although the West Point cadets beat the Gators 20–8, the Florida team, also nicknamed "the Orange Blossom Terror" for its fierce play, earned much respect that season, which ended in a fine 6-1-2 record.

Robert "Ark" Newton, pictured here running off-tackle, arrived at UF in 1921 from his native Arkansas (hence his nickname) and became a member of the football team, after Coach Van Fleet saw him kick a 60-yard punt. In one game, he kicked a 92-yard punt. Newton was also a strong runner and receiver.

A powerful runner on the 1923 team was Ed Jones, seen here in the open field. Captain Van Fleet, one of the Army's greatest commanders, coached the 1923 and 1924 teams to a record of 12-3-4 against the likes of then-powerhouses Georgia Tech and Alabama. Van Fleet would become a four-star general, serving in both world wars, including the D-Day landings in World War II, and the Korean War. He lived to the age of 100 and is buried in Arlington National Cemetery.

Because freshmen were not allowed to compete against varsity teams in the Southern Conference, they had their own intercollegiate schedule. The "Baby Gators" went undefeated in 1926 and were called "Champions of the South" at a time when the Gator varsity had a poor 2-6-2 record, the only time that decade that they did poorly.

Around 1926 Ulmer Hawkins of Tampa presented to UF the Hawkins Trophy. School officials were to inscribe on the base of the trophy the names of the Gator players who made the mythical All-Southern football team.

The Great Depression had many effects on UF, including scaling back the grandiose plans involving University Auditorium, built in 1927. Even at that, the auditorium became the center of campus, especially after the 1953 construction of the nearby Century Tower, with its magnificent carillon at the top. At the base of the tower for many years was a pen that enclosed a live alligator.

The 1927 varsity included Dale Van Sickel (fourth from right, seated), an All-American the next year, and D. K. Stanley (second from left, seated), who would coach the Gators from 1933 to 1935. The head coach from 1925 to 1927 was Tom Sebring, who attended law school while coaching and later became chief justice of the Florida Supreme Court and then dean of the Stetson University Law School.

UF's first football All-American was Dale Van Sickel (sometimes misspelled Sickle). He played offensive end on the 1928 team, as well as defense, averaging almost 60 minutes a game. After college, he went to Hollywood, founded the Stuntmen's Association of Motion Pictures, and performed in more than 300 movies, including the Marx Brothers' comedy *Duck Soup*.

The 1928 Gators led the nation in scoring, totaling 336 points to their opponents' 44 and beating Georgia for the first time. UF's only loss that 8-1 season was to Tennessee on a soggy field in Nashville, a game in which some Gator fans thought the groundskeeper had soaked the gridiron to slow down the high-scoring Florida team.

One of the most lopsided victories of the 1928 season or any season was the 71–6 victory over Sewanee in Jacksonville in November. This photo shows Gator runner Goodbread on a 24-yard touchdown run. After the first three games, all the rest were away, including Jacksonville, Savannah, and Knoxville. Florida won seven of the nine games played against Sewanee, a rivalry reaching back to 1914.

These women at a Florida homecoming game in the late 1920s were part of a long-continuing tradition, begun in 1924, of having graduates return to campus, renew acquaintances, attend a football game, and brag of their success. They would be introduced during halftime in pageantry that became more and more elaborate.

Coach Charles Bachman (at far-left) was the eighth head coach of the Gators. Over his five seasons (1928–1932), he built a 27-18-3 record and was the first Gator coach to be inducted into the National Football Foundation and the College Hall of Fame. He later became the football coach at Michigan State University for 14 years.

Early broadcasters of Gator games sat between the fans and the gridiron. Seen behind these four announcers at a 1928 game are (left to right, beginning with the third person) Governor Doyle Carlton, Mrs. John Tigert, Senator Duncan Fletcher, Mrs. Doyle Carlton, and UF president John Tigert.

The year 1929 was hard in Florida, with the stock market crash and diseases that wiped out the orange crop, but at least exciting football games took the minds of many off the serious problems facing the country. UF's 1929 team triumphed with an 8-2 record, including a victory over Oregon in Miami, the first time the Gators had played a West Coast team.

A New Stadium and Hard Times

(1930–1945)

When university officials opened the new Florida Field in 1930, many hoped it would be the beginning of continued success on the ball field as well as in the classroom. John Tigert III had become president of the University of Florida in 1928, and he would lead the school through the next 20 years, troubled times for the country in general and Florida in particular.

Not only would the state and nation suffer economic collapse in the Great Depression, but the onset of World War II in 1941 would deprive the state and university of thousands of young men who were drafted into the Armed Services. The Gators' first game in the new stadium, a loss to powerhouse Alabama at homecoming, was a portent of the next two decades as resources grew tight, tourism slacked off dramatically, and higher education seemed like a luxury to many Floridians who were barely eking out a living.

Fortunately for the University of Florida, President Tigert was the right person at the right time for the helm. As the former head of the athletic department and head football coach at the University of Kentucky, he had a strong interest in sports and knew how effective a strong athletic program could be in the education of college students. He was a member of the National Rules Committee for college sports, helped rewrite the rulebook for football, and helped establish the Southeastern Conference, which UF joined and helped elevate to a high level of play.

The mediocre success of football coaches in that era (Bachman, Stanley, Cody, and Lieb) was a disappointing 78-81-8, but the strong academic foundation built by President Tigert would attract outstanding faculty, better and better students, and the beginnings of the road to becoming the flagship of the state system of higher education. The fact that so many Florida legislators were graduates of UF led to the legislature's insistence on excellence in the classroom and on athletic fields. The stage was set for the next step toward achieving that excellence.

Florida Field was dedicated on November 30, 1930. Nearly 22,000 fans attended the first home game, a loss to Alabama 20–0, in a facility that would be expanded as the team improved. The announcer for the game was a UF student, the famous Red Barber, who would become a baseball announcer for the Reds, Dodgers, and Yankees.

Although the 1930 homecoming game against Alabama was a Florida loss, the women in the Homecoming Court and their ROTC escorts had good seats near the field. That loss was only one of three for the Gators that season. They finished with a 6-3-1 record, outscoring their opponents 198–61. The one tie was a 0–0 defensive match against the hated Bulldogs of Georgia.

End Ed Parnell of Stuart (no. 85 in the first row), who captained the 1931 football team, received honorable mention on the All-Southern Conference team in a year when the Gators had a disappointing 2-6-2 record. The decade would not be good for Florida football, which finished the ten years with a poor 42-52-6 record.

The first game of the 1931 season, an away contest against North Carolina State in Raleigh, ended in a 34–0 victory for the Gators, who had an effective passing and running game. The rest of the season turned out poorly, a 2-6-2 record and being outscored by the opposition, 168–74. The Gators, in fact, were shut out by three teams: Alabama, Georgia Tech, and UCLA.

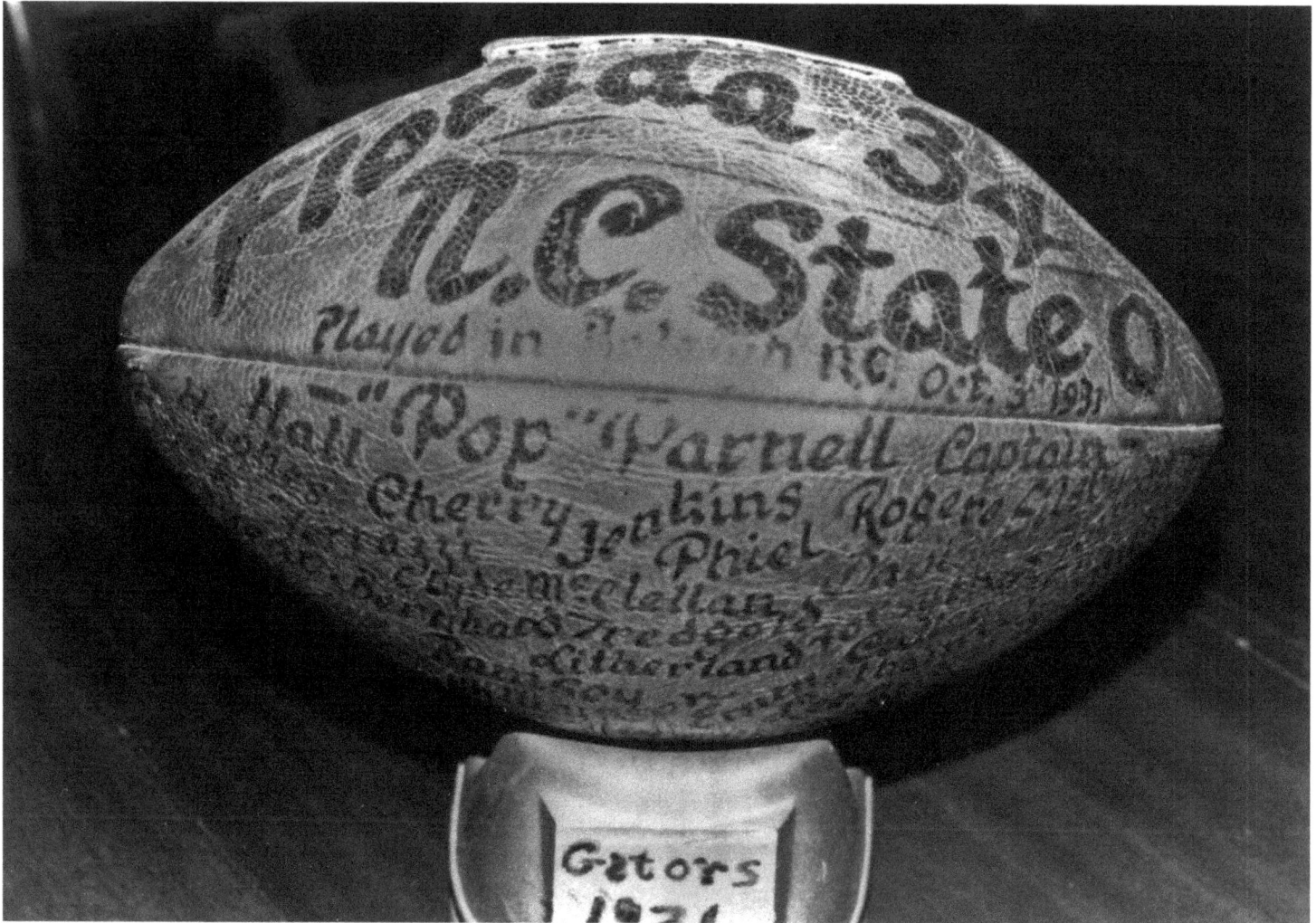

The Gators kept the game ball showing their victory against North Carolina State, 34–0, in 1931. The Gators traveled a lot that season, going to North Carolina, New York, Alabama, and California to play their games. Such travel to out-of-state, hostile stadia gave them good experience and also allowed local high school players to see the kind of football played by the Gators.

On October 31, 1931, the Georgia Bulldogs played the Gators at Florida Field for the first time, defeating them 33–6. The Bulldogs would not return to Gainesville until 1994, when the stadium in Jacksonville, where the two teams usually played each other, was being renovated for the NFL's Jacksonville Jaguars.

Dr. John Tigert, former head football coach at the University of Kentucky and UF's president since 1928, had an architect design the stadium, not in a normal oval, but with three straight sides on the north, west, and east. Unlike many stadia, Florida's did not have a track surrounding the playing field.

Walter "Ben" Clemons played center for the Gator football and basketball teams in the early 1930s. He also pitched for and captained the 1930 baseball team. Such multi-sport athletes would be common at Florida, into the present day. Permission to play two or more sports at UF was a strong recruiting tool used by the coaches.

Cheerleaders in the 1930s were all white males at a time when the university did not have any African-American or female students. The six students pictured here also served as the executive committee for the Gator Pep Club. The cheerleaders were usually skilled gymnasts who could leap and do breathtaking cartwheels.

Many students, including athletes, went to the campus infirmary for minor aches and bruises, colds, and shots. The building, officially known as the Students Health Center, opened in 1931. In later years Shands Hospital, down the hill from the campus, would treat the more serious illnesses among students.

In October 1934, two American Legion officers joined Governor David Sholtz (second from left) and UF president John Tigert (third from left) to dedicate a plaque on the north wall of Florida Field during the Tulane game. A scroll behind the plaque listed those Floridians killed during World War I.

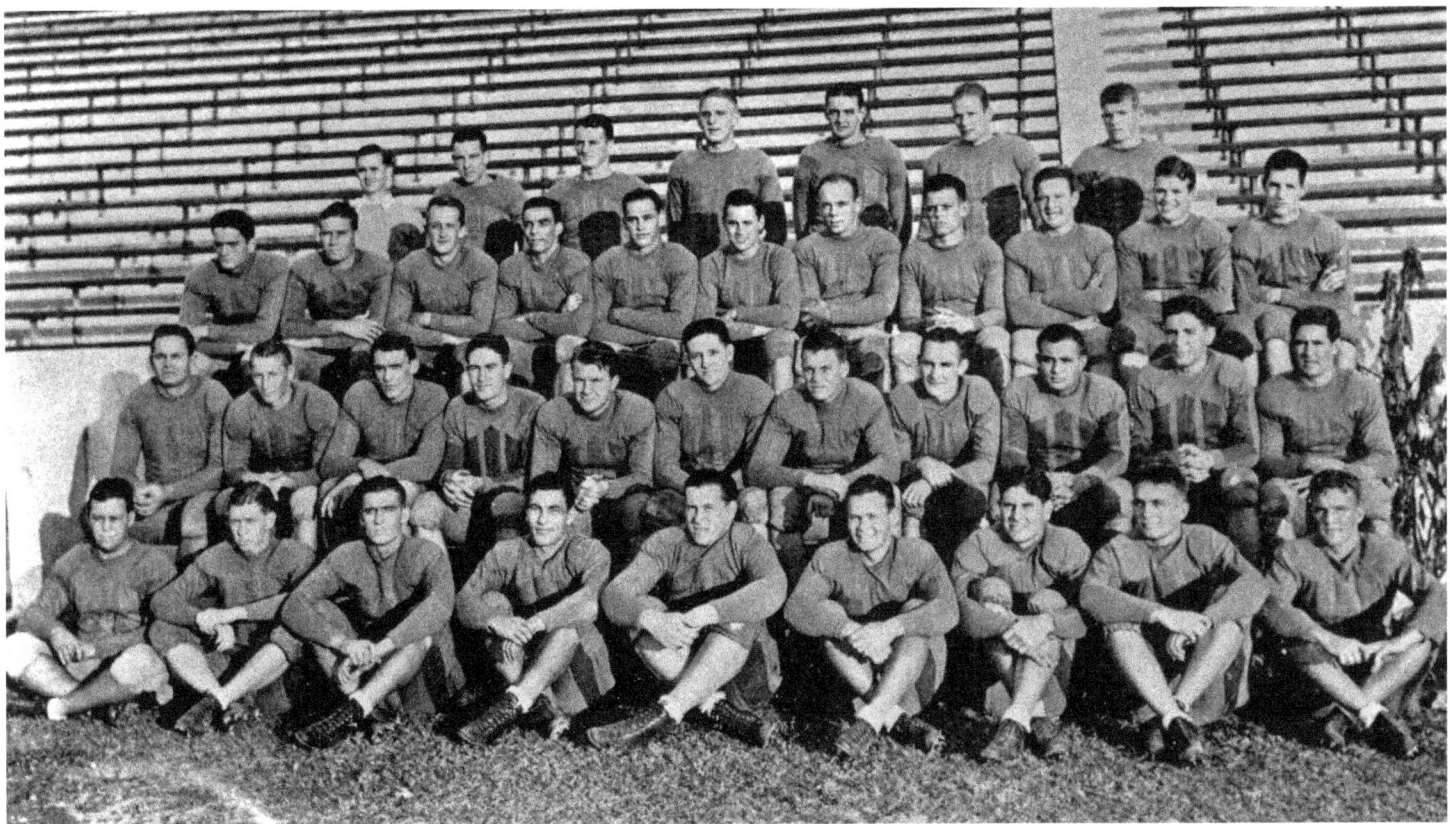

The 1935 team posted only a 3-7 record, but in their three wins that season against Stetson, Sewanee, and South Carolina, the Gators scored 76 points and held the opposition scoreless. The poor record that year led to the firing of Coach Stanley. He would be replaced by Coach Josh Cody from Vanderbilt University in Nashville.

Despite a well-maintained playing field and enthusiastic crowds on game days, the Gators did so poorly in the last half of the thirties that Coach Josh Cody, the school's tenth head coach, could manage only a 17-24-2 record over four seasons (1936–1939). Cody would become one of six coaches hired to lead the Gators in the 1930s and 1940s.

The so-called Freshman Pep Squad sat together at football games in the 1930s. Over the years various customs involved all the freshmen—for example, saying "hello" to everyone they met on campus, memorizing the names of university and student government officials, and not taking shortcuts across the Plaza but using only the sidewalks and roads. The cheerleaders would sometimes call all the freshmen out to join in impromptu pep rallies and pajama parades.

The George Peabody Foundation gave UF a $40,000 gift in 1913 to help establish a College of Education. Peabody Hall, pictured here in the mid-1930s, was one of four academic buildings in the center of campus, the others being Anderson, Flint, and Floyd halls. For many years Peabody Hall was the scene of classes for those students, including athletes, who trained to become teachers.

UF managed to hire Josh Cody from Vanderbilt University as the team's tenth head coach, but he struggled in the years just before World War II, managing only a 17-24-2 record for one of the worst winning percentages of any Gator head coach. His four seasons (1936–1939) were very forgettable.

As a tailback–defensive back, Walter "Tiger" Mayberry was Florida's first All-SEC player (1937). The Daytona Beach native served in World War II as a Marine Corps fighter pilot. He was shot down and captured by the Japanese in 1943 and died in a Japanese prisoner-of-war camp, becoming one of seven UF football players killed in action during the war.

Against one of its perennial foes, the Auburn Tigers, the Gators pulled off a major upset at a 1938 game played at Municipal Stadium in Jacksonville under inclement conditions of rain and very cold weather. Behind the pinpoint passing of quarterback Bud Walton and a blocked punt for a safety, the UF team won, 9–7.

When Coach Pop Warner's Temple University team came to Gainesville in 1938, the Gators faced one of the game's greatest coaches in the final year of his 44-year coaching career. Temple won the game, 20–12, and one of the Owls' runners (shown here) returned a Florida kick-off for 103 yards, the longest ever at Florida Field.

When the Gator football team showed up in Massachusetts to play a strong Boston College team in 1939, some Florida students brought along a live alligator in a blanket and then handed it to a reluctant BC cheerleader. The victory over the BC team, 7–0, was one of the highlights of a poor season, which ended with a UF record of 5-5-1. It would be Coach Josh Cody's last season as head coach of the Gators.

Workers installed lights in the football stadium in the late 1930s, thanks to a generous donation from Georgia Seagle, a strong supporter of the university. The lights enabled homecoming events (as pictured here) and, later, football games to take place in the cool of the evening, thus avoiding daytime heat and humidity, although Gator teams were hardened to such conditions.

Forrest "Fergie" Ferguson started at offensive and defensive end for three years (1939–1941) and became the second Gator All-American football player. He served in the U.S. Army during World War II, dying in 1954 of wounds he had suffered during the 1944 invasion of Normandy. He was one of the best players of all time for UF.

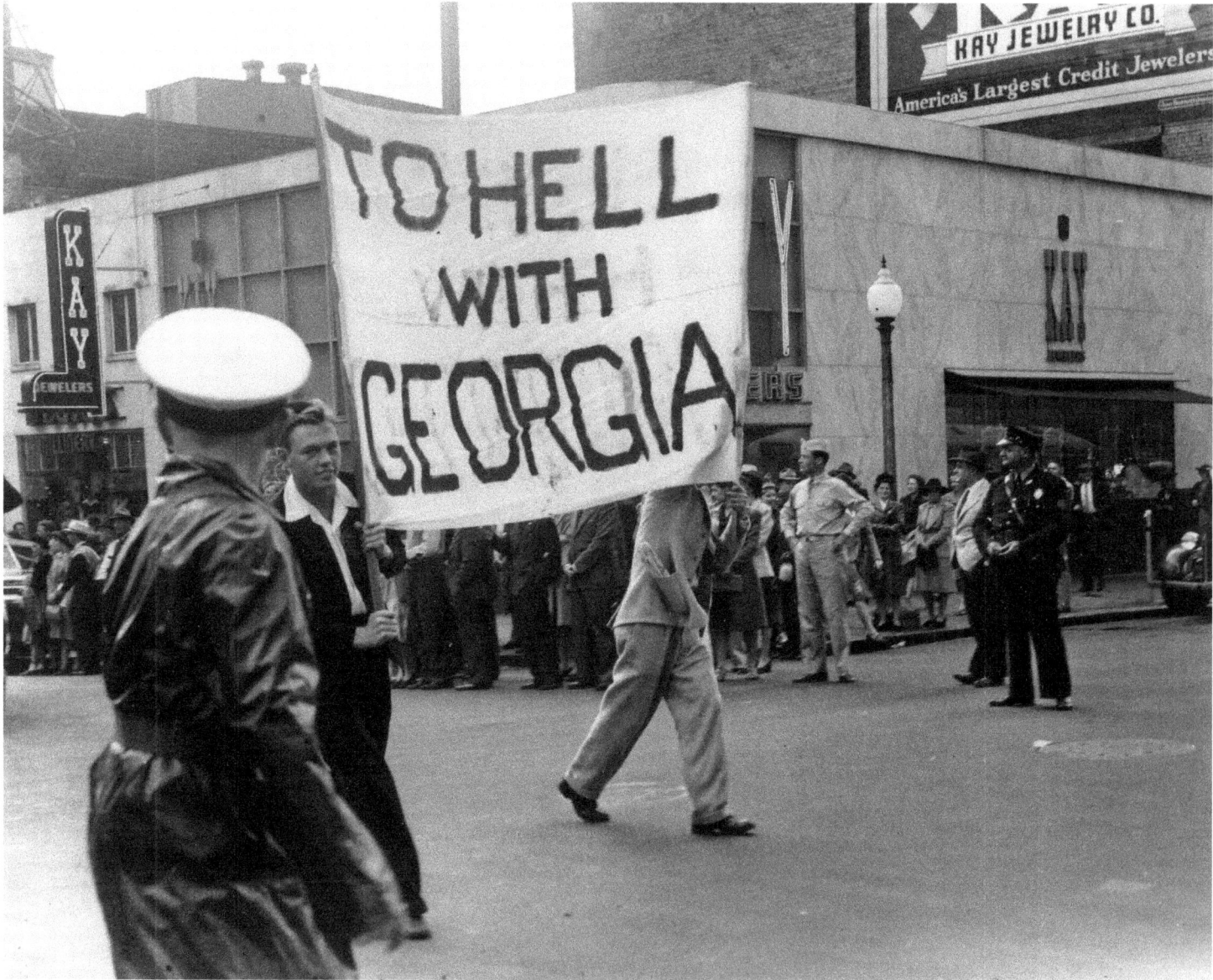

The annual game against the Georgia Bulldogs, usually played in neutral Jacksonville, is one of the fiercest rivalries in the Southeast, especially because both teams are in the same division of the Southeastern Conference and their game is usually held late in the season, when the division championship is on the line.

Photos of cheerleaders appeared in the school's annual yearbook, *Seminole,* which students produced from 1910 until 1973 and then again beginning in 1983 with a new name, *The Tower,* to prevent confusion with Florida State University in Tallahassee, which had a Seminole Indian as its mascot.

UF president John Tigert (at left) and Dean Harold Hume of the College of Agriculture rode onto Florida Field in 1943 in style. That year the Gators, like many college teams in America, did not field a football team, because World War II was in progress. Many male students were drafted during the war, and seven UF football players were killed in action.

Coach Tom Lieb was the head football coach at UF from 1940 to 1945 (excluding the war year 1943), but left with a losing 20-26-1 record. He was, however, the first Gator coach to beat both Georgia and Georgia Tech in the same season, his first. Two years later, Georgia beat Florida 75–0 in Jacksonville in one of the worst Gator defeats ever.

Postwar Success

(1946–1969)

The retirement of President Tigert in 1946 and the selection of J. Hillis Miller to be UF's fourth president in 1947 marked the end of straitened circumstances for the country and the state. Thousands of ex-GIs returned home, many of them determined to earn college degrees. Pressure to admit women to the University of Florida led to the enrollment of both men and women in 1947, and that would lead to an enormous boom in student numbers and a dramatic change in the school's offerings, including athletics.

The establishment of both the J. Hillis Miller Health Center (named after President Miller) and Shands Hospital (named after a UF football player and state legislator) led to a great influx of construction money and federal grants and—more important—to the growing reputation of UF as the educational and health capital of the state.

On the football field, the school recruited two coaches (Wolf, Woodruff) before hiring the immensely successful and popular Ray Graves in 1960. Graves coached the school's first Heisman Trophy winner (Steve Spurrier) and introduced a wide-open passing game (with quarterbacks Spurrier and John Reaves) that fans would come to expect.

School officials would keep expanding the football stadium to try to meet the increasing demand for tickets, especially as the success of the team attracted more and more superior athletes, tougher schedules, radio and television revenue, and greater national exposure to football fans nationwide.

In 1946, after World War II and before large numbers of veterans arrived to help, UF suffered its worst season ever, going 0-9-0. In this game against Villanova, the Gators lost 27–20 at home. Not until Charley Pell's first year as head coach (1979) would the year be as bad, when the Gators lost all ten games, though tying one.

In 1947, two years after World War II ended and after thousands of soldiers returned home, many armed services personnel, both men and women, wanted to take advantage of the G. Bill, which enabled them to attend college. UF became coeducational, and the athletic teams recruited men and women to lead the cheers.

The Fighting Gator Band became a regular fixture at football games in the late 1940s and led the fans in rousing fight songs. UF's band had a proud tradition of service, dating back to 1917, when the U.S. entered World War I against Germany. When the worldwide conflict erupted, the university band joined the war effort as a unit, becoming the 124th Infantry Band.

Coach Raymond "Bear" Wolf, head football coach for four seasons (1946–1949), welcomed many older players as returning veterans joined the team. The Florida legislature helped fund athletic scholarships to UF through tax revenues generated from pari-mutuel betting at racetracks and jai-alai frontons in the state.

The small scoreboard in the south end zone lasted from the 1930s to the 1960s, but would later be replaced with a huge sign that gave much information about downs, yards to first down, time-outs, and total statistics. Workers would later add temporary bleachers to the south end zone to increase its capacity to more than 62,000.

One of Coach Wolf's best players was Chuck Hunsinger (no. 46), who started for the Gators for four years (1946–1949) and had some great moments, among them winning SEC Back of the Week for the 1949 Gator victory over Georgia. He was part of a surprisingly intact squad that stayed together for three years (1946–1948) and had a role in a great upset: a 7–6 win over North Carolina State in 1947.

Chuck Hunsinger (no. 46) was very popular with the fans and was willing to sign autographs after a game.

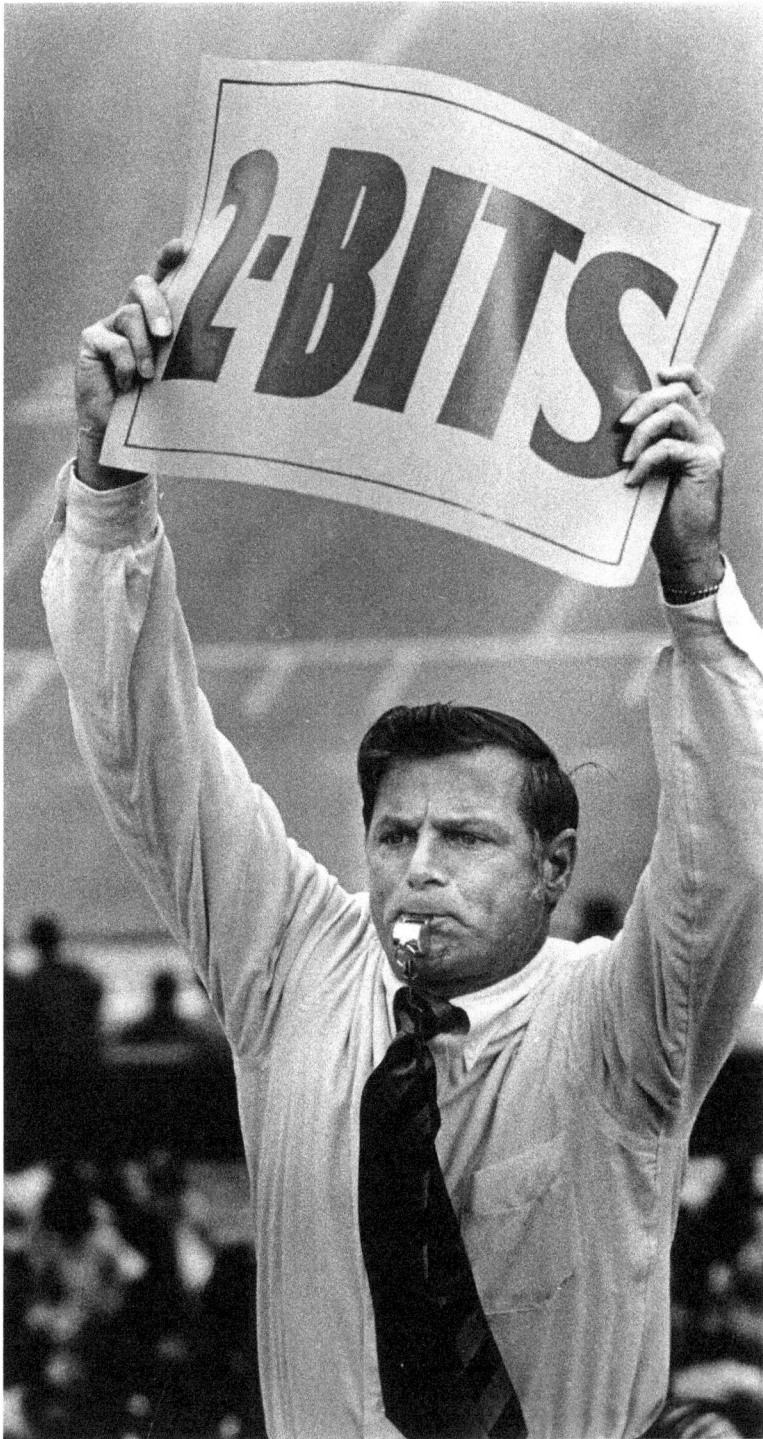

Beginning in 1949, George Edmondson, Jr., of Tampa, Florida, better known as Mr. Two Bits, would go to the center of Florida Field dressed in his yellow shirt with orange-and-blue tie and lead the crowd in a "two bits" cheer.

Coach Wolf is shown here with Fred Montsdeoca on the left and Jimmy Kynes on the right in 1949. Kynes, UF's first All-SEC lineman, was the last Gator player to play 60 minutes in a football game and, in fact, averaged 55 minutes a game that season. Measuring a big 6 feet 3 inches, 204 pounds, Kynes, who lettered for four years (1946–1949), became a lawyer and in 1964 the youngest Attorney General of Florida.

In a game against Auburn that ended in a tie in Mobile, Alabama, in Coach Wolf's last season as head coach (1949), he is seen speaking with 21-year-old end Fal Johnson of Gainesville. Many of the players were in their mid-20s, having served as soldiers in World War II. Alumni pressure at the end of that season led to his resignation, to be replaced in 1950 by Bob Woodruff.

Choosing an alligator for mascot, shown here in an early form, turned out to be a pretty good idea. It would give rise to things like a nickname for Florida Field. In the 1990s, the stadium was dubbed "the Swamp," the place where gators live and eat animals like bulldogs and wildcats.

University of Florida

FIGHTING GATORS

FLORIDA 'GATORS

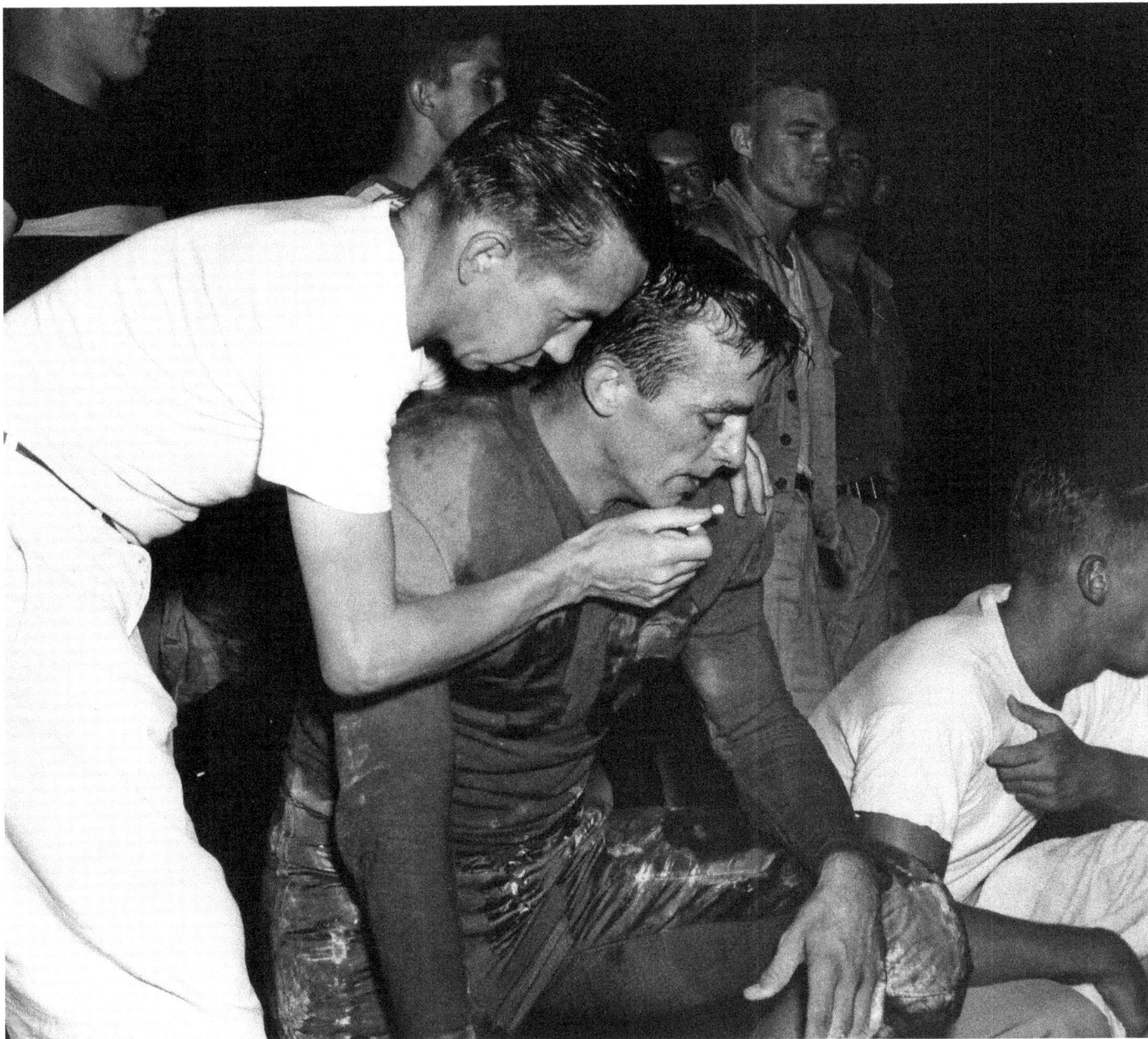

Medical assistance was often quite basic in the games of the 1940s, in this case a quick dose of smelling salts to revive a woozy Gator. The lack of strong, protective gear led to more injuries than in games today, and some players, like Jimmy Kynes, played all 60 minutes of a game, a tactic that could exhaust the less physically fit.

Chuck Hunsinger (no. 46), seen here with Coach Wolf, had a great 1949 season, running for 774 yards and scoring 12 touchdowns. He was so good that an Alabama reporter composed "The Hunsinger Song" about him with these words: "Hunsinger the Humdinger you ought to see him go!" After college, the Chicago Bears drafted him in the first round for the NFL.

The 1949 win against Georgia, 28–7, ended a seven-game losing streak against what has consistently been one of the fiercest rivalries of the Gators. Coach Wolf's players carried their beleaguered coach off the field on their shoulders before 27,000 fans in Jacksonville. It would be Wolf's last victory in a 4-5-1 season, his last. His four-season record was a disappointing 13-24-2.

The Fightin' Gator Band, which attended all home games and many away games, would grow from several dozen to more than one hundred musicians.

An aerial view of the UF campus in the late 1940s shows the football field in the middle of a track field, baseball diamond, tennis courts, gymnasium, and a newly begun Florida Gym, where the basketball team would play for 31 seasons (1949–1980). Generous benefactors donated money for the installation of lights around the football field and for the construction of off-campus housing for the athletes.

The main library, pictured here in 1949, remained one of the centerpieces of a beautiful campus. The success of the football team helped the library in later, leaner years when the Athletic Association donated to the library some of the money earned in bowl games, thus allowing all the students to benefit from the success of the team on the field.

Adding upper levels to the stadium in 1950 ushered in the Bob Woodruff decade as the school's 13th head coach. He built a record of 53-2-6 in ten seasons, led UF to its first-ever bowl game (a victory over Tulsa in the 1952 Gator Bowl), beat the Georgia Bulldogs six of ten games, and started the UF-FSU rivalry.

Students in the stands have always enjoyed participation, such as performing card pictures at the command of an announcer. These pictures faced the alumni, who sat in the shaded section of the stadium, with a view of the pictures like that of the photographer.

The fifties saw a growing awareness of good training, eating, and exercise. Head trainer Sam Lankford (at far-right) and his staff are shown here taping the ankles of players for an early morning practice before the student-athletes head to class. The training room in the Florida Gym would eventually become state-of-the-art.

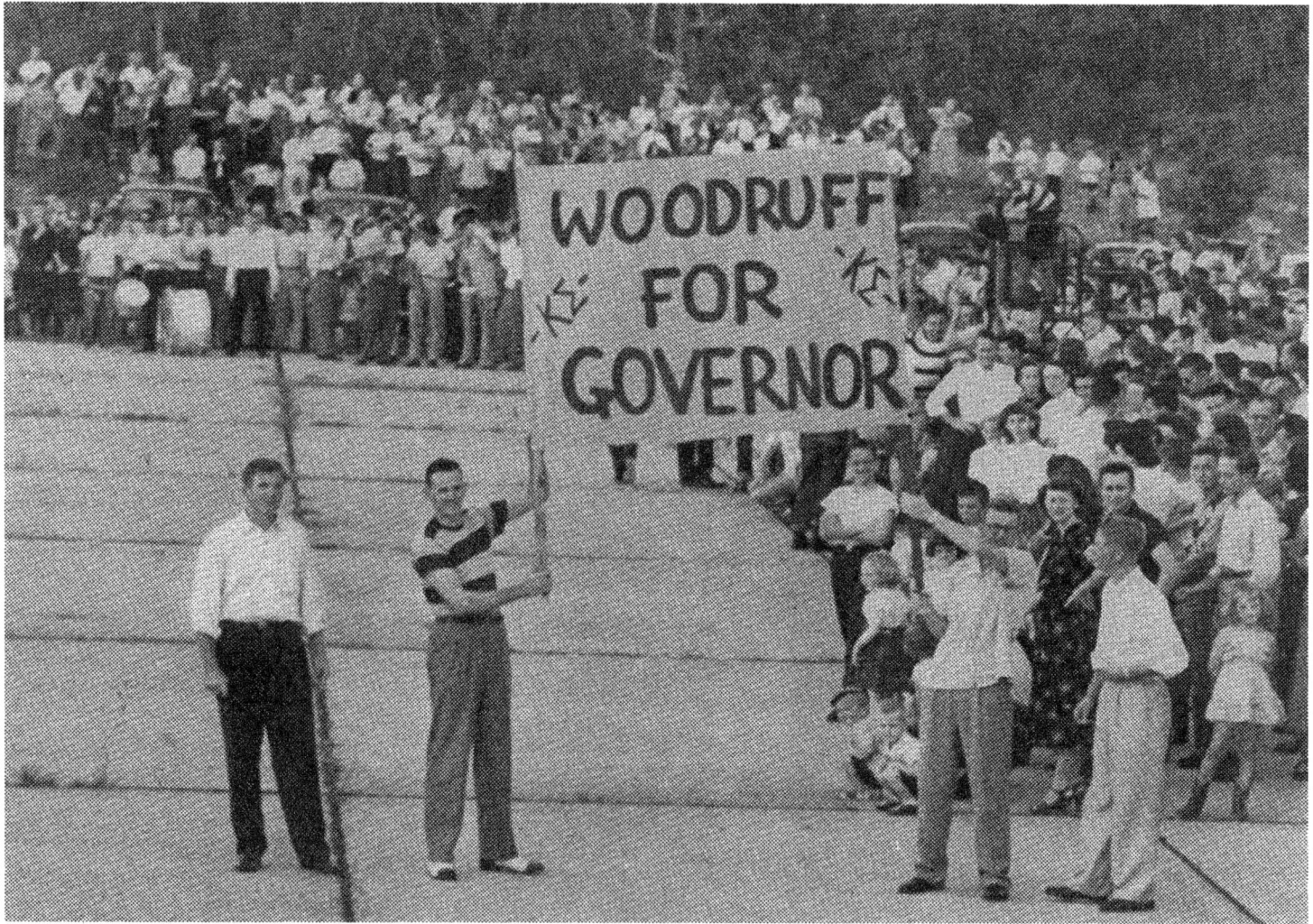

When the 1950 Gator team upset the favored Vanderbilt team in Nashville, 31–27, many fans met the returning team at the Gainesville airport and held up signs like this one. It would be one of the few times until the modern era that fans supported their coach so strongly. That season would end in a disappointing 5-5 record when the team lost its last four games.

One of the new traditions in the Coach Woodruff era was the ringing of the so-called Victory Bell after an important win, for example the 1950 win over Vanderbilt. The bell was salvaged from the USS *Florida*, a battleship commissioned in 1911 and scrapped in 1932. Officials placed the bell in the Hub, which was in the center of campus.

The sidelines of football fields during the 1940s and 1950s slowly became better equipped to handle the physical bruises and injuries suffered by the players. Equipment included oxygen masks and liniments, to help prevent serious injuries.

Coach Woodruff, having been coached as a Tennessee player by defensive-minded Bob Neyland, emphasized defense, for example in this 1950 game, when the white-helmeted Gators beat Furman 19–7. Although Woodruff's teams won more games than any other Gator team up to that time (1953), by the end of the decade fans wanted more offense.

The 1950 team had three quarterbacks: (from left to right) Haywood Sullivan, Angus Williams, and Kent Stevens. The 6-foot-4-inch Sullivan became the first sophomore in the SEC to pass for more than 1,000 yards. The Boston Red Sox baseball team signed him after his sophomore season with a $75,000 bonus, and he left for the pros.

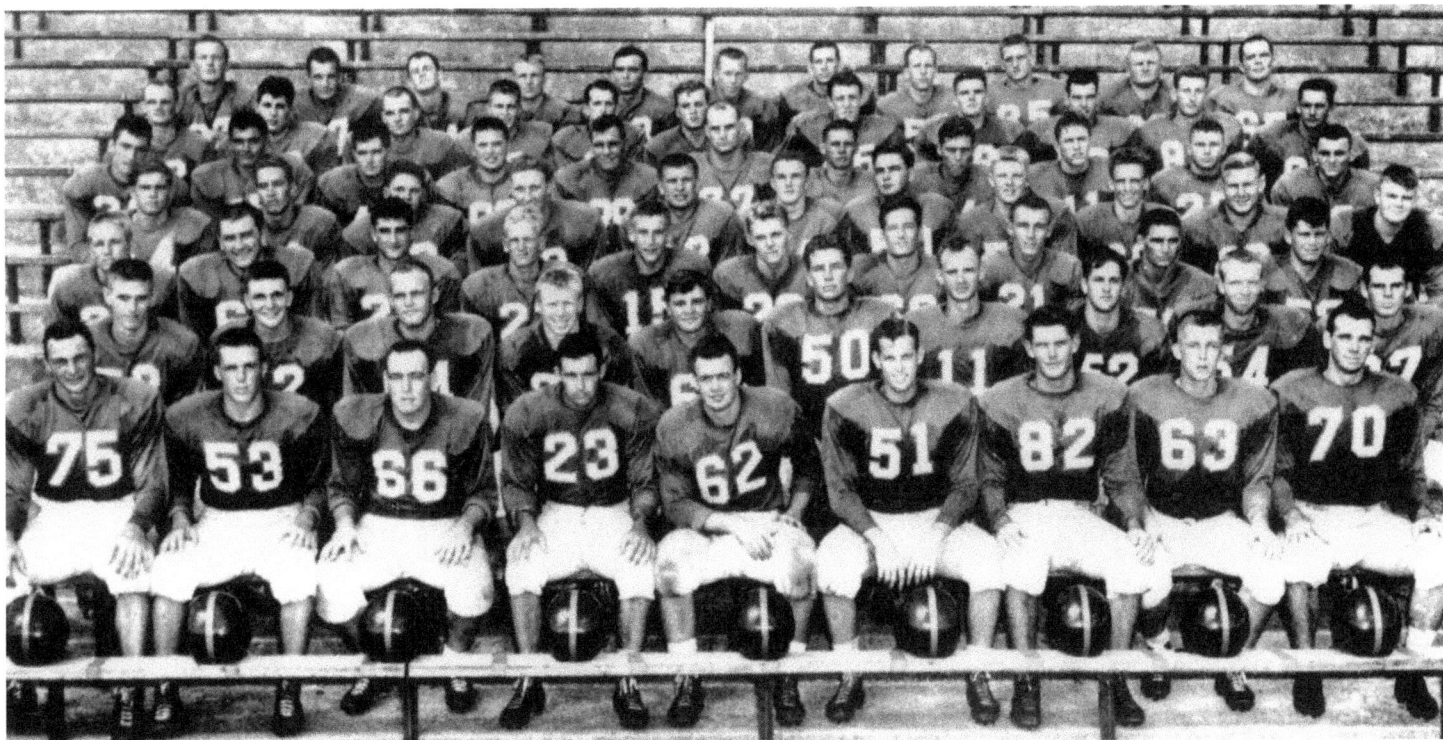

The outstanding defensive lineman on the 1952 varsity was Charlie LaPradd (no. 75, at far-left in the front row), a former Army paratrooper in World War II and a relatively old football player at 24. LaPradd was an All-American who played both offense and defense, leading the team to its first bowl game: a win over Tulsa in the Gator Bowl.

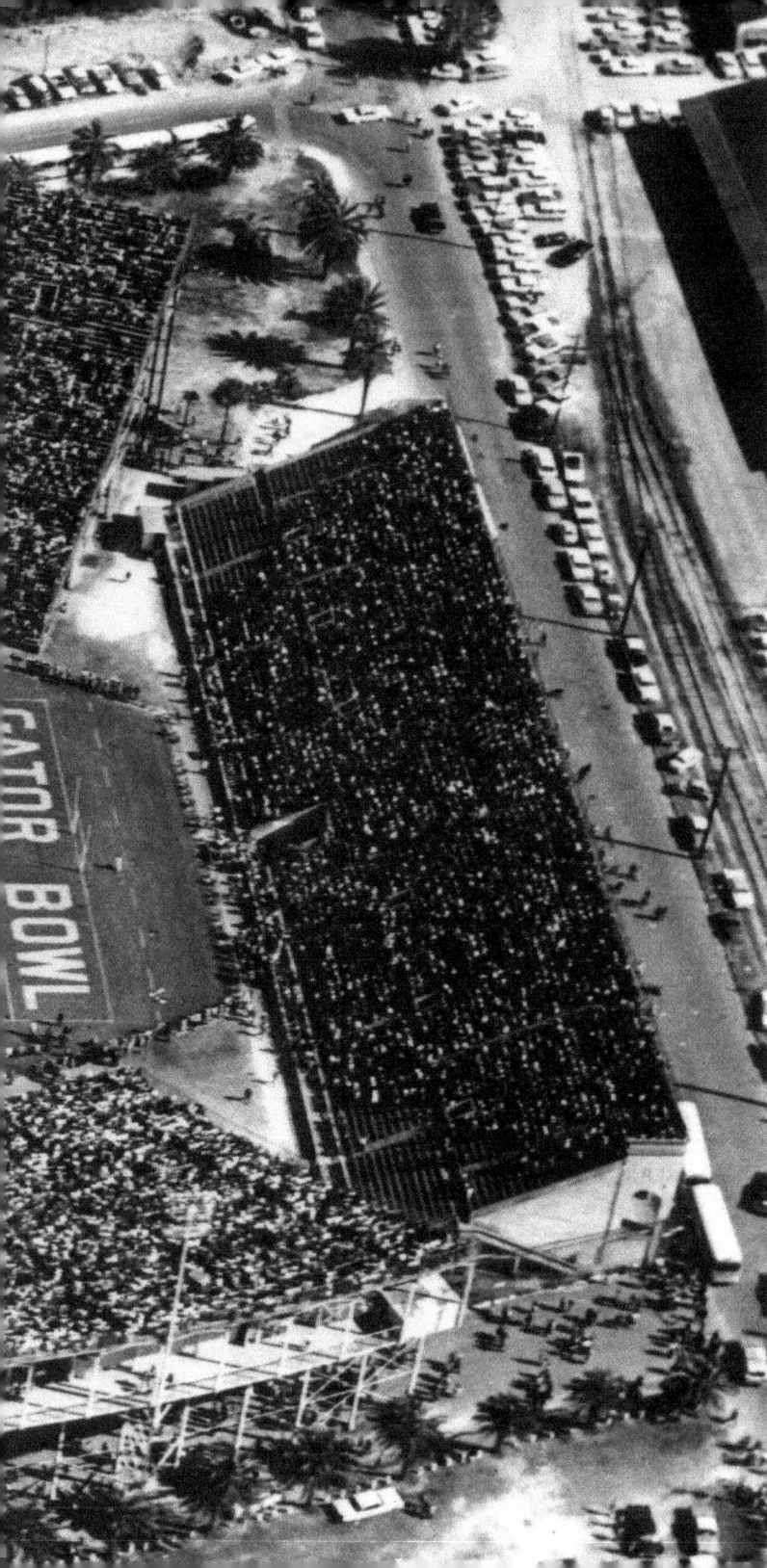

Jacksonville's Gator Bowl has been a favorite out-of-town place for the Gators to play. The Gators played eight bowl games there between 1953 and 1999, winning six times, including the school's first bowl ever, the 1953 win over Tulsa.

The homecoming parade, held the day before the big football game, proceeded east on University Avenue from the stadium to the center of town. Thousands of spectators lined both sides of the street to see the bands, floats, and personages, such as Miss Florida for 1954, who waves to the crowd from a convertible.

The 1956 Gators, pictured here in their coats and ties, held a very good 6-3-1 record, a 28–0 thrashing of Georgia, a five-game winning streak, and a national ranking of number 12. The five-game winning streak was the longest up to that time following the eight straight wins of the 1928 team, the one that led the nation in scoring.

Defensive guard John Barrow, a first-team All American, was also the SEC Lineman of the Year in 1956. After UF, he played football for 15 seasons in the Canadian Football League and then became general manager at Toronto. As would frequently happen at UF, his son, Greg, joined the team and lettered as a tackle in 1980.

A live alligator has occasionally come out of the waters on campus and wandered around, much to the delight of students and broadcasters in town, in this instance for an episode of the *Hootenanny* TV show. Lake Alice, just south of the football stadium, is still a favorite swimming hole for the animals.

Vel Heckman, who lettered for three years as a Gator (1956–1958), became a first-team All-American defensive player when the Football Writers' Association chose him an All American for *Look* magazine in 1958. He joined other great players under Bob Woodruff, among them Rick Casares, Jimmy Dunn, Don Fleming, and Joe D'Agostino.

An aerial view of the UF campus from the late 1950s reveals its great size, with the athletic fields concentrated on the western edges and the health center to the south.

After much reluctance on the part of UF officials to play the Seminoles of Florida State University, but urged on by state legislators and by Governor Leroy Collins, UF agreed to play the new team in 1958 in Gainesville. The program cover for the first game implied a friendliness that was not present on the field.

The Gators beat the Seminoles 21–7 in their 1958 match, mostly because UF quarterback Jimmy Dunn, seen here receiving the MVP award, ran for two touchdowns and made a defensive stop on an FSU player about to score. The Seminoles tried one surprise play, a tactic that both teams would use in the years to come.

The 1960s at UF saw the hiring of a new head coach, the beloved Ray Graves, who instituted a powerful offense, recruited the school's first Heisman Trophy winner (Steve Spurrier), and established a winning tradition at the school with a record of 70-31-4 that decade. He took the Gators to five bowl games, winning four of them.

Cheerleaders in a 1960 home game at Florida Field found a new use for their megaphones. In later years, fans in the stands would not be allowed to use umbrellas, which could drip water on nearby spectators and could be used to smuggle in liquor.

The equipment in the press box in the early 1960s was basic: a microphone, telephone, binoculars, stat sheet, and food. In later years, the press box would be enclosed and have state-of-the-art facilities.

UF quarterback Larry Libertore, who weighed just 135 pounds, passes over an FSU defender blocked by fullback Don Goodman (no. 45). "Little Larry" Libertore, a cagey option runner-passer, led the Gators to a record nine wins in 1960. When Tommy Shannon replaced Larry as signal caller, Larry became a defensive back.

In his first season as head coach, Ray Graves took his team to play Baylor in the 1960 Gator Bowl in Jacksonville. Their victory was the first of four bowl games his team won that decade. The pageantry of the bowl games as pictured here played well on television and for the fans there in person.

Three lovely coeds pretend to corral a gator on campus. Among the very few other schools that used an alligator for a mascot were Allegheny College in Pennsylvania, San Jacinto College in Texas, San Francisco State University in California, and Green River Community College in Washington. The original mascot of San Francisco State University was the Golden Gate Bridge, and the teams were nicknamed the "Gaters," which eventually became the "Gators."

After three straight wins over the Seminoles, UF tied them in 1961. Here assistant head coach Gene Ellenson (at left) pretends to fight with FSU head coach Bill Peterson over the Governor's Cup, given to the winner of the annual intrastate game. The first six games between the two schools were played in Gainesville, and the contest traveled to Tallahassee only after FSU improved Doak Campbell Stadium.

Ray Graves posed with his coaches and team during the 1962 season, one that ended with a 7-4 record, including a 17–7 win over Lambert Trophy winner and eastern football power Penn State in the Gator Bowl. During that season Coach Graves heard from his brother in Knoxville, Tennessee, about a local young man up there who would put Gator football on the map to stay: Steve Spurrier.

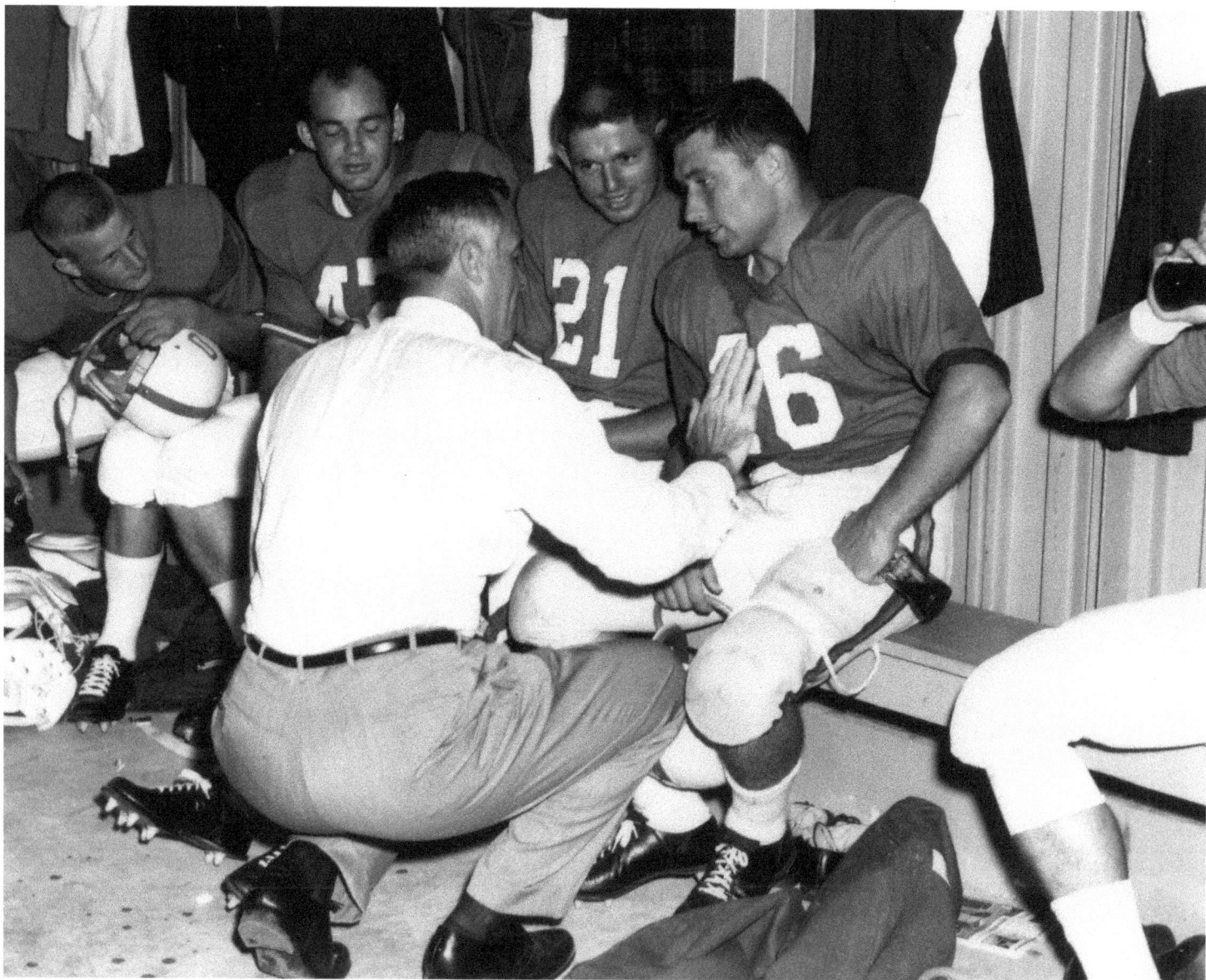

Coach Graves, seen here talking with quarterback Mike McVay (no. 16) and halfback Don Deal (no. 21) during a game in the early 1960s, had much experience in football, having played at Tennessee in college and then with the Philadelphia Eagles in the NFL and having coached at Tennessee and Georgia Tech.

Each fall right before homecoming, student groups, including sororities and fraternities, spend much time building elaborate displays for the Friday afternoon parade. This particular photo shows the display built by Alpha Gamma Rho in 1962. That year's theme dealt with the space race that President Kennedy initiated at his inauguration in 1960.

Charlie Casey, seen here running for a touchdown against Richmond in 1963, was one of Steve Spurrier's favorite targets for a pass in the early sixties. Casey earned first-team All-America honors for his 58 receptions, 809 yards gained, and 8 touchdowns scored in 1965. He was one of UF's best receivers ever.

What had to be one of the least fearsome of gator outfits was used in the early 1960s by the UF cheerleaders. How UF became the Gators dates back to 1908, when a local Gainesville merchant was visiting his son in Virginia, wanted to have pennants made for UF's team, decided on an alligator because of its association with Florida, and the rest is history.

In 1964, Larry Dupree became the first Gator running back to earn first-team All-America honors. His 1,725 rushing yards in three years is one of the highest totals ever for a Gator. He was the captain of the 1964 team, which posted a 7-4 record, scored 181 points, and held their opponents to only 98.

In 1964, sophomore Steve Spurrier (no. 11) and senior Tommy Shannon (no. 12) shared the duties of quarterback. Tommy "T-Bird" Shannon, who had shared the same duties with Larry Libertore in 1962, became the MVP in Florida's 1962 Gator Bowl win over the highly favored Penn State Nittany Lions. He later became a successful businessman in Florida.

In a 1964 game, quarterback Steve Spurrier (no. 11) ran behind Larry Beckman (no. 66), Marquis Baeszler (no. 34), Randy Jackson (no. 88), Bill Carr (no. 51), and Jim Benson (no. 60). Beckman, Benson, Carr, and Spurrier made the All-SEC team at least once in their careers at Florida. Spurrier won the 1966 Heisman Trophy, the first Gator to do so.

After Franklin "Pepper" Rodgers (to the left of Coach Ray Graves in this photo) served as an assistant coach at UF, he went on to become the head coach at the University of Kansas, UCLA, and Georgia Tech. At Kansas he led the team to the 1968 Big 8 championship. He also coached the Memphis Showboats of the United States Football League.

Steve Spurrier was not only a great quarterback, but also an effective kicker. Seen here kicking a punt against Southern Methodist University in the first game of the 1964 season, he is well known for the winning, 40-yard field goal against Auburn in 1966, effectively clinching the Heisman Trophy as a senior.

Steve Spurrier finished the 1965 season by being named the most outstanding player in the Sugar Bowl, the first time a player from the losing team had won that honor. He broke six bowl records in that game, a 20–18 loss to Missouri. The following season he helped the Gators beat Auburn by kicking a field goal near the end of the game.

In a clever publicity shot, the photographer put Spurrier the player on the shoulders of two of his coaches, whereas normally the players carried their successful coach off the field after a great victory.

When the Gator coaches noticed how weak the ballplayers were after practice, Dr. Robert Cade, Dr. Dana Shires, Dr. H. James Free, and Dr. Alejandro de Quesada at UF helped develop Gatorade as a way to restore blood sugar and electrolytes to the players and therefore their strength and endurance. The popular noncarbonated sports drink, manufactured by the Quaker Oats Company, went on to earn UF millions of dollars in royalties.

Bill Carr lettered at UF for three years (1964–1966), started at center in 32 consecutive games, and earned All-American honors in his senior season. The New Orleans Saints in the NFL later drafted him, but an ROTC commitment prevailed and he served in the U.S. Army in Korea. Carr became UF's athletic director from 1980 to 1986.

One of the most controversial UF-FSU games was played in Tallahassee in 1966, when the field judge called Seminoles' receiver Lane Fenner (no. 82) out-of-bounds on this catch late in the game. The Gators held on to win, 22–19, in what has come to be called "the Lane Fenner Game." Debate still rages about that game.

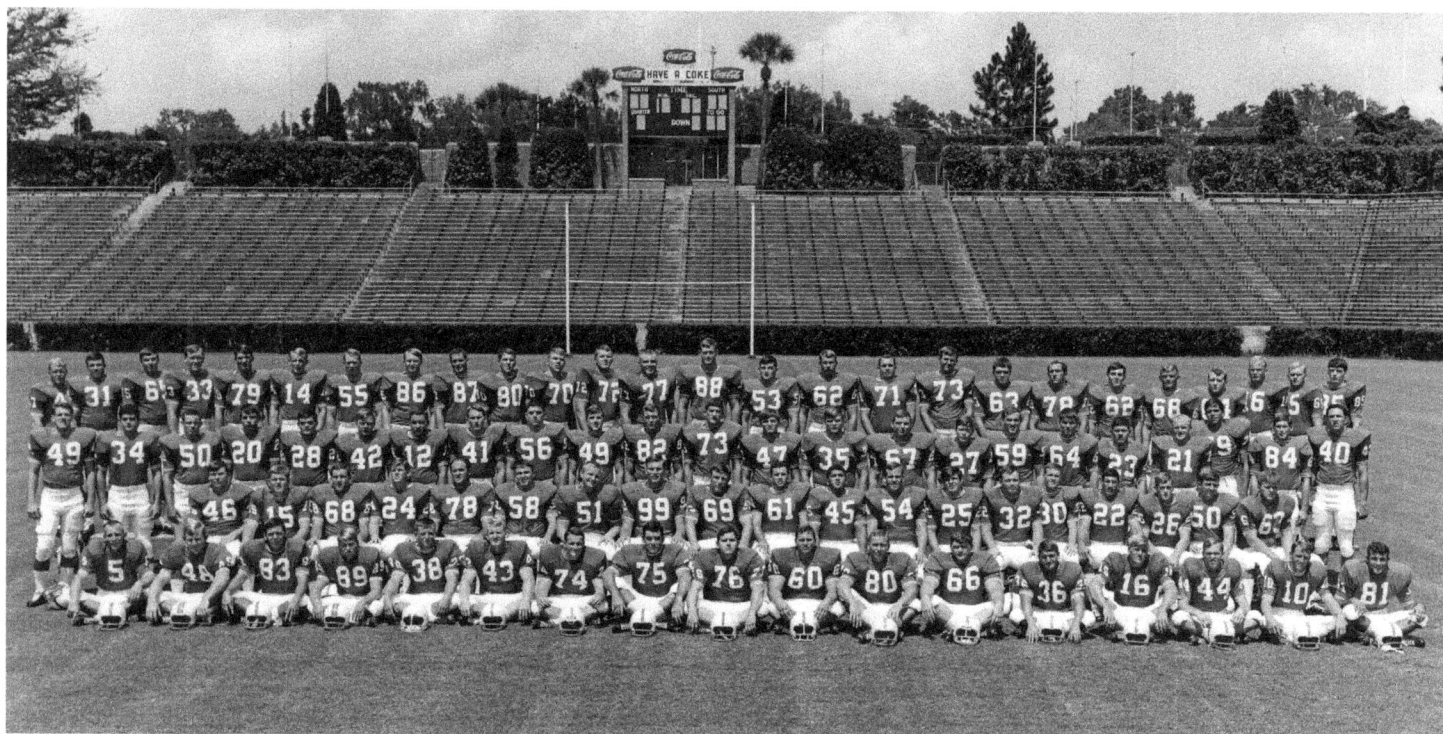

One of the best players on the 1967 varsity was no. 44, Richard Trapp (third from right in the front row). In his three seasons with the Gators (1965–1967), he set the SEC career record with his 132 catches, 1,783 yards, and 10 touchdowns. In 1967, he earned first-team All-SEC honors with his 58 catches for 708 yards.

Jim Yarbrough (no. 88) blocks for Tom Christian (no. 31) in 1967, a disappointing year for the team, which finished 6-4. Yarbrough lettered for three years (1966–1968), was named to UF's Team of the Century as a tight end, and later played in the NFL (1969–1977) as an offensive tackle for the Detroit Lions and Houston Oilers.

In the 1967 Orange Bowl in Miami, the Gators beat Georgia Tech 27–12 in the final game of the Yellow Jackets coached by Bobby Dodd (the former coach of Ray Graves). Gator tailback Larry Smith rushed for a 94-yard touchdown, still a record for the Orange Bowl. Smith rushed for 187 yards that day and was named the MVP of the game.

In 1968, fullback Larry Smith (no. 33) was very effective for battering the line and gaining short yardage, in this case against FSU for a 9–3 win. He and guard Guy Dennis were named All Americans that year, but the Gators managed only a 6-3-1 season. The next season would be the last coaching that Coach Graves would do.

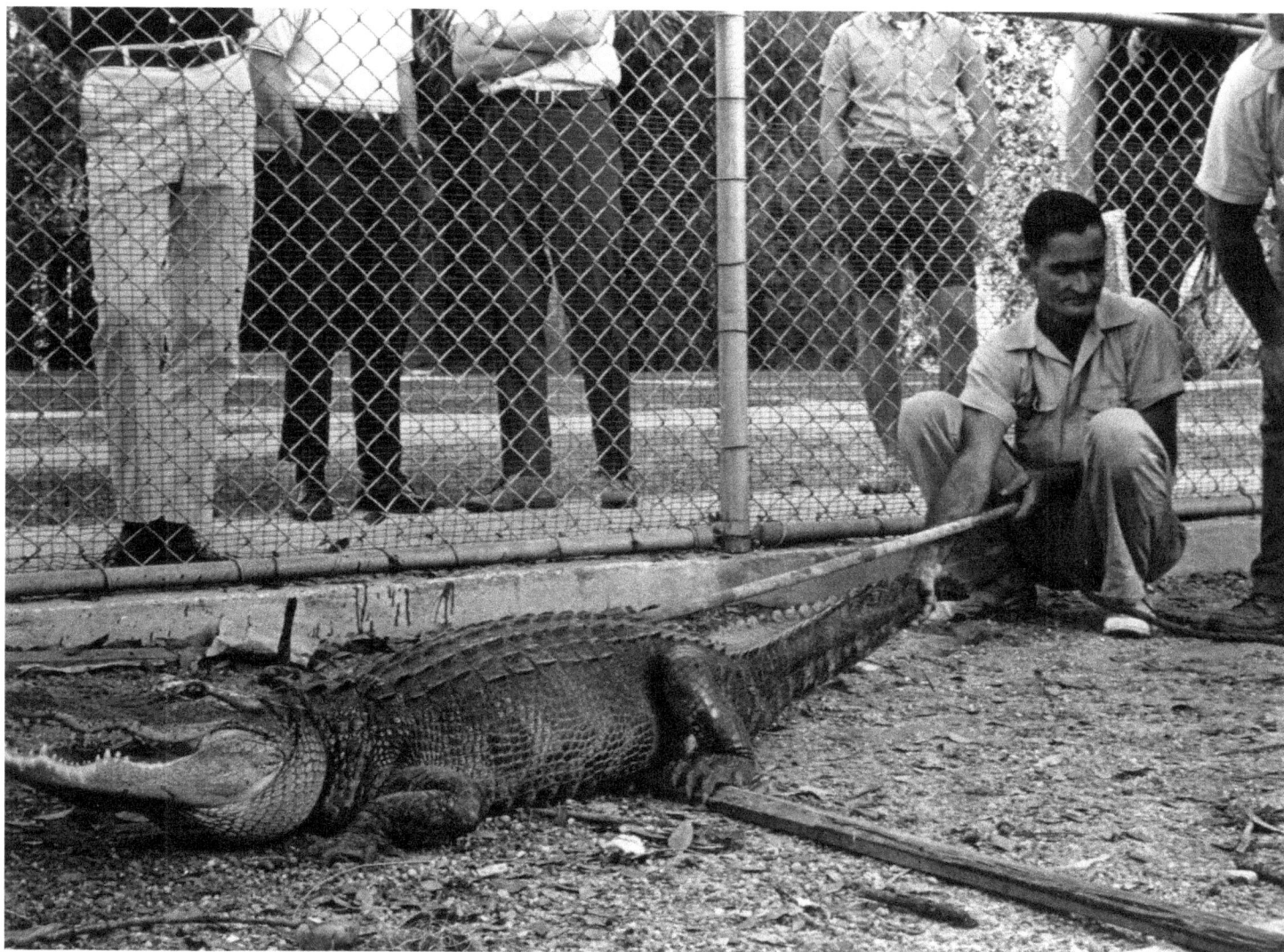

For many years, a live alligator was kept in a pen near Century Tower. After opposing fans foolishly entered the pen to paint the animal in the school colors of the opponent, officials wisely removed the reptile to Lake Alice to live out its life in peace. Using an alligator as a mascot may have inspired Coach Spurrier to nickname Florida Field "the Swamp."

On the third offensive play of the 1969 season, UF quarterback John Reaves threw a touchdown pass to fellow sophomore Carlos Alvarez, starting a 9-1-1 season in which the Gators scored 329 points, the second-highest record in UF history to that time, while holding opponents to just 187. It would be the end of a great decade of Florida football.

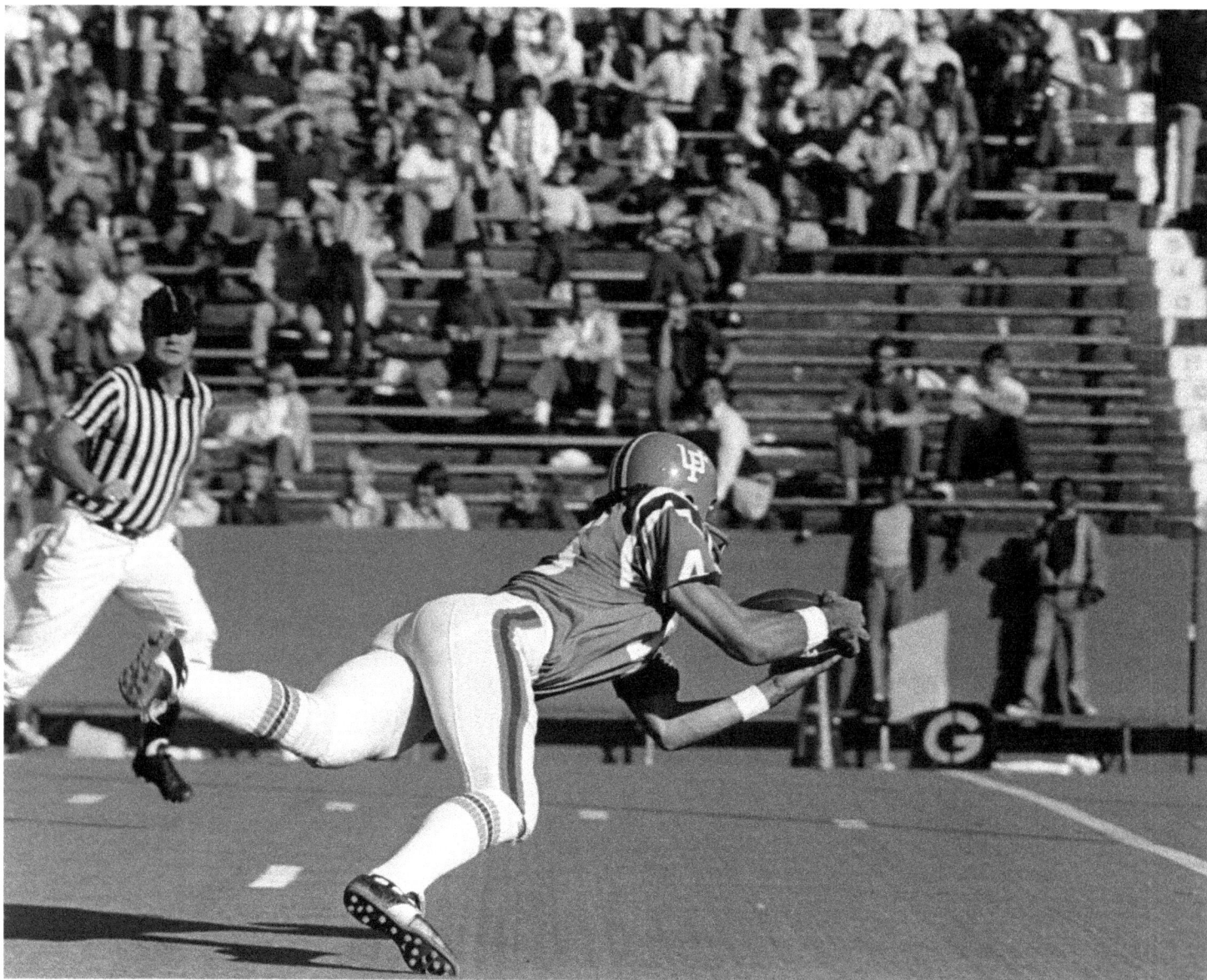

Carlos Alvarez, nicknamed the "Cuban Comet," set Gator football records that stood for decades. His first Gator reception from John Reaves on the third play of the opening game against Houston, which had been ranked number one in the pre-season, was for a touchdown in a lopsided UF victory, 59–34.

The Auburn Tigers were particularly strong at home at Cliff Hare Stadium, for example in beating the Gators. In the 1969 game there, the Tigers intercepted Gator quarterback John Reaves nine times in thumping the Gators 38–12 for their 12th straight victory there. A touchdown pass to UF's Bill Dowdy (no. 84) was one of the few bright spots that day for UF.

Norm Carlson, pictured here in 1964, earned a bachelor's degree at UF (1956), worked in Atlanta as a sportswriter (1956–1959), and served as Auburn University's sports information director (1959–1963) before beginning work at UF, where he became the sports information department's knowledgeable historian.

The governors of Florida, such as Claude Kirk, shown here in 1969, often attended college football games in the state, but had to adopt a neutral stance during intrastate clashes, for example between UF and FSU, since each school had thousands of alumni throughout the state.

Defensive back Steve Tannen, who played for the Gators for three seasons (1967–1969), was a two-year All-SEC choice, the top defensive back in the SEC (1969), and an All American (1969). He was particularly effective in blocking punts and intercepting passes. After UF, he played in the NFL for the Jets (1970–1974) before becoming an actor in Hollywood.

President Stephen C. O'Connell was a "stand-in dad" for a player at a 1969 ceremony honoring the parents of the seniors. A long tradition at UF was for the senior players to be accompanied by their parents at the last home game, giving the fans one more chance to acknowledge the players for their long hours of practice and contributions to the team.

By the 1960s, the equipment on the sidelines had become better organized and complete as the teams grew in size and as medical doctors stood by in case of an emergency.

DISAPPOINTMENTS AND TRIUMPHS

(1970–1996)

When Coach Ray Graves resigned and Doug Dickey became the head football coach in 1970, Florida fans hoped that the former Gainesville native and Gator quarterback would continue the wide-open offense of the sixties. But the conservative play-calling of Dickey and a succession of disappointing, conservative coaches (Charley Pell, Galen Hall, Gary Darnell) left many fans disgruntled and yearning for more.

NCAA penalties slightly derailed the success of the team and finally led to the demand for the return of Steve Spurrier, the school's first Heisman Trophy winner and the genius of the fun-'n'-gun offense that lit up scoreboards and earned the school its first national championship and second Heisman Trophy. Upset victories over traditional powers like Alabama, Penn State, Georgia Tech, and Auburn put UF on the athletic map for good. Increasing revenues from radio and television brought in much money to the athletic teams, and the generous contributions of the Athletic Association, a private entity, to summer teaching, library resources, and the building of the Academic Advisement Building helped all the students and faculty.

Integration of the athletic teams, begun by football coach Graves, and of the university as a whole, attracted student-athletes of all races. The post-college success of football players like Pat Summerall, Cris Collinsworth, Scot Brantley, Emmitt Smith, and Danny Wuerffel brought good recognition to the University of Florida, attracted better and better students and faculty, and helped in raising money during the school's endowment campaigns.

All of that would spell increasing success in the post-1996 age, when Coach Urban Meyer became the head coach (in 2005), Tim Tebow won the school's third Heisman Trophy (in 2007), and the Gator football team won two national championships.

Florida Field, which was becoming one of the finest facilities for football games in the Southeast, saw a different style of play in the 1970s. The wide-open, passing offense of Ray Graves in the 1960s became more of a running game as new coach Doug Dickey introduced the wishbone offense. The 1960s would be missed by Florida fans.

Guard Burton Lawless lettered at UF for three years (1972–1974), became a first-team All American (1974), and was named to UF's Team of the Century. After UF, he played for the Cowboys (1975–1979), the Lions (1980), and the Dolphins (1981) in the NFL.

The school's band grew larger and larger over the years until it included more than a hundred performers, baton girls, and flag wavers. By the 1970s, members spent much time practicing and could often be heard for a mile or so around the stadium early on home-game days.

Coach Dickey's first win as the head coach was against Duke in Jacksonville, 21–19. The closeness of the contest caused much consternation on the sidelines as is clear from the looks on the faces of these coeds.

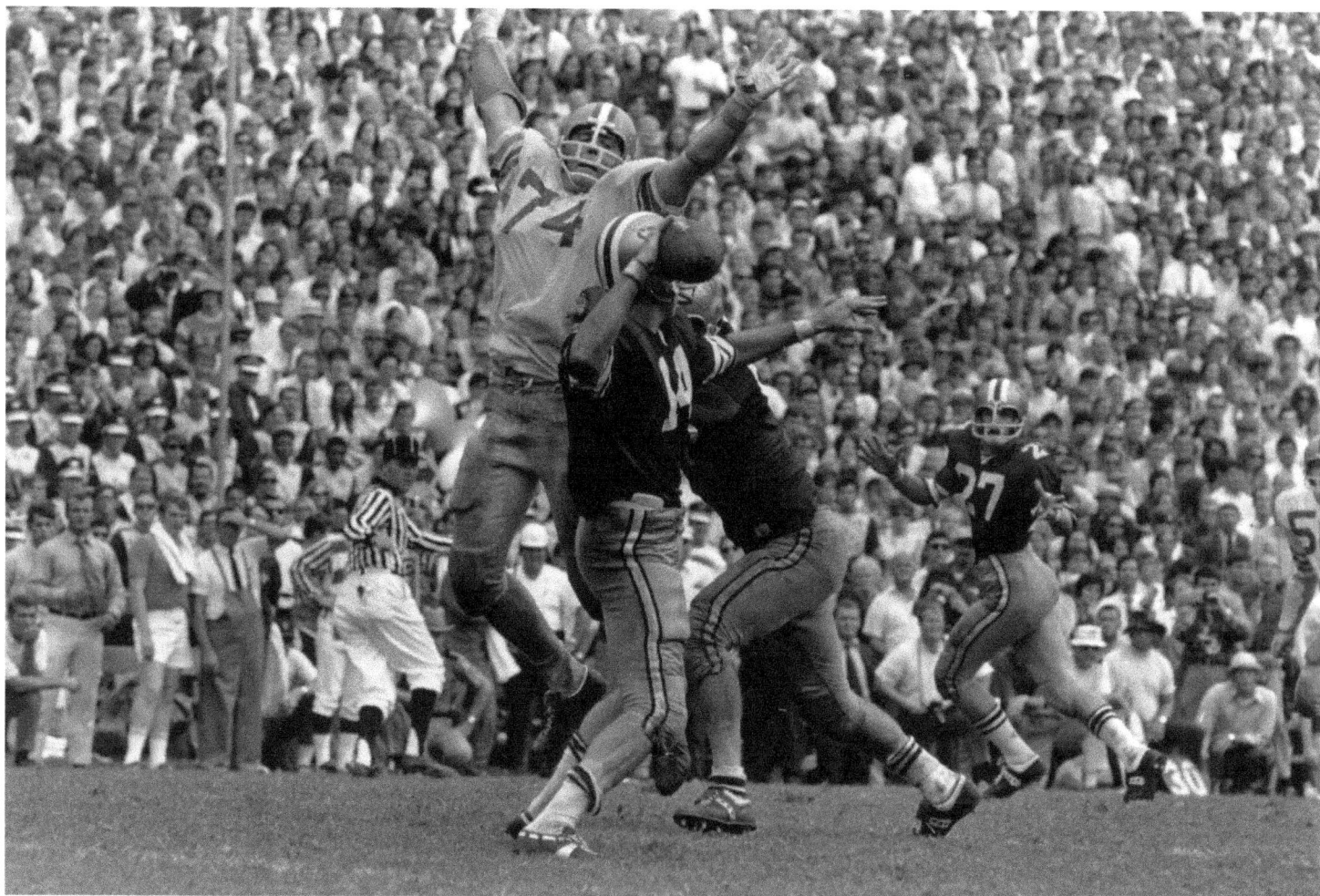

Jack Youngblood (no. 74), considered by many to be UF's best defensive end, was a first-team All-American player in 1970. After his Gator career, he was drafted by the NFL's Los Angeles Rams in the first round and played his entire career with that team (1971–1984). He was an All-Pro seven times and is best known for playing in Super Bowl XIV with a broken leg.

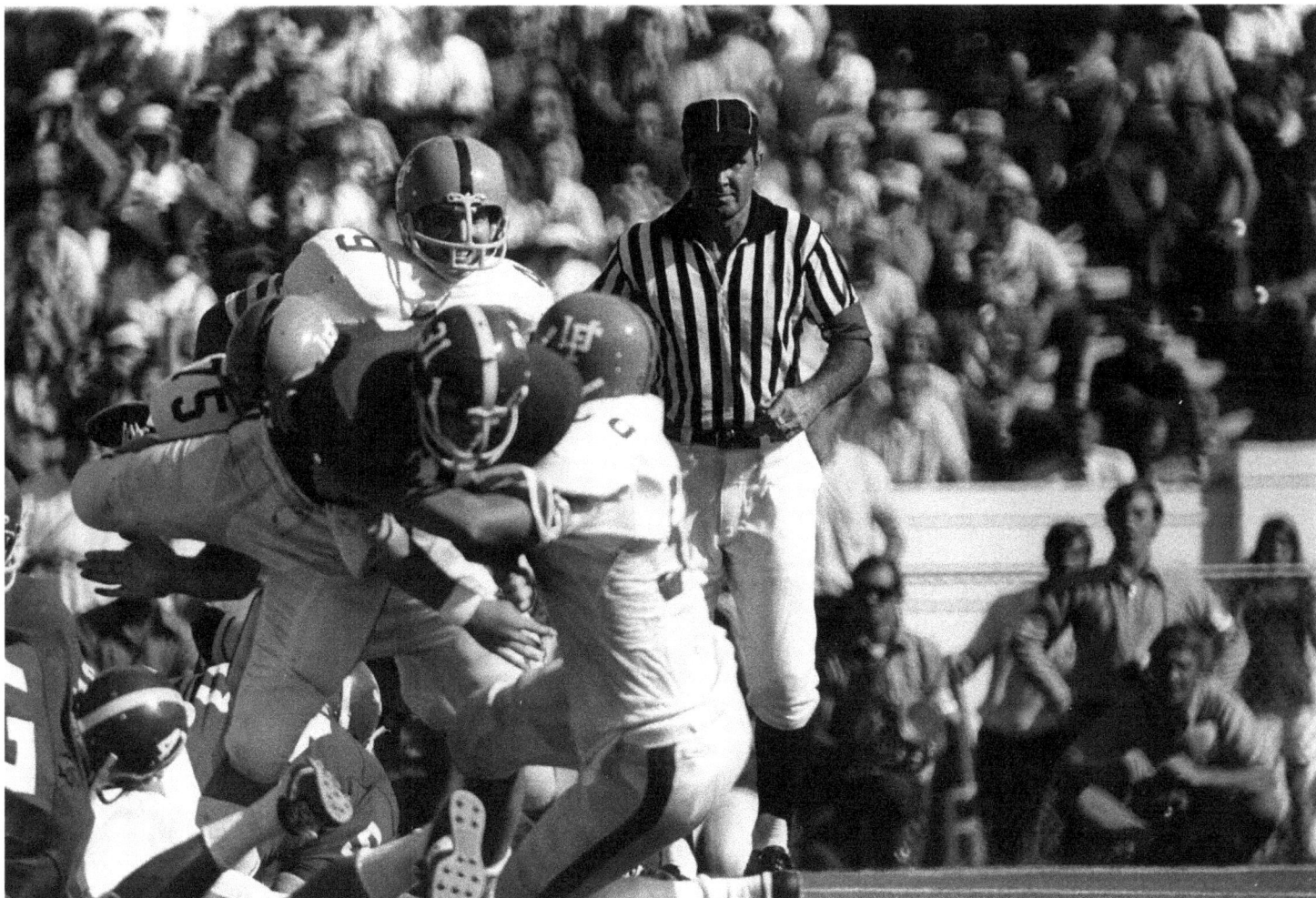

Coach Dickey's first loss as the head coach was in Tuscaloosa against the Crimson Tide of Alabama, 46–15. He would go on to a 7-4 record that season, but the losses were against SEC rivals Alabama, Tennessee, and Auburn, as well as the independent Miami.

Tommy Durrance (no. 33) was a three-year starter at halfback for the Gators (1969–1971) and a good transition from the Graves era to the Dickey era. He led the team in rushing for two seasons, scored a record 30 touchdowns in his career (thus his nickname "Touchdown Tommy"), and was the unanimous choice to be captain of the 1971 team.

A transfer from Miami-Dade Junior College, Nat Moore set the UF rushing record in 1972 with 145 carries for 845 yards and 9 touchdowns. As a senior he broke his knee early in the next season, but returned to his great form when he carried the ball against FSU 15 times for 109 yards in a 49–0 rout of the Seminoles, the worst defeat that team had ever suffered.

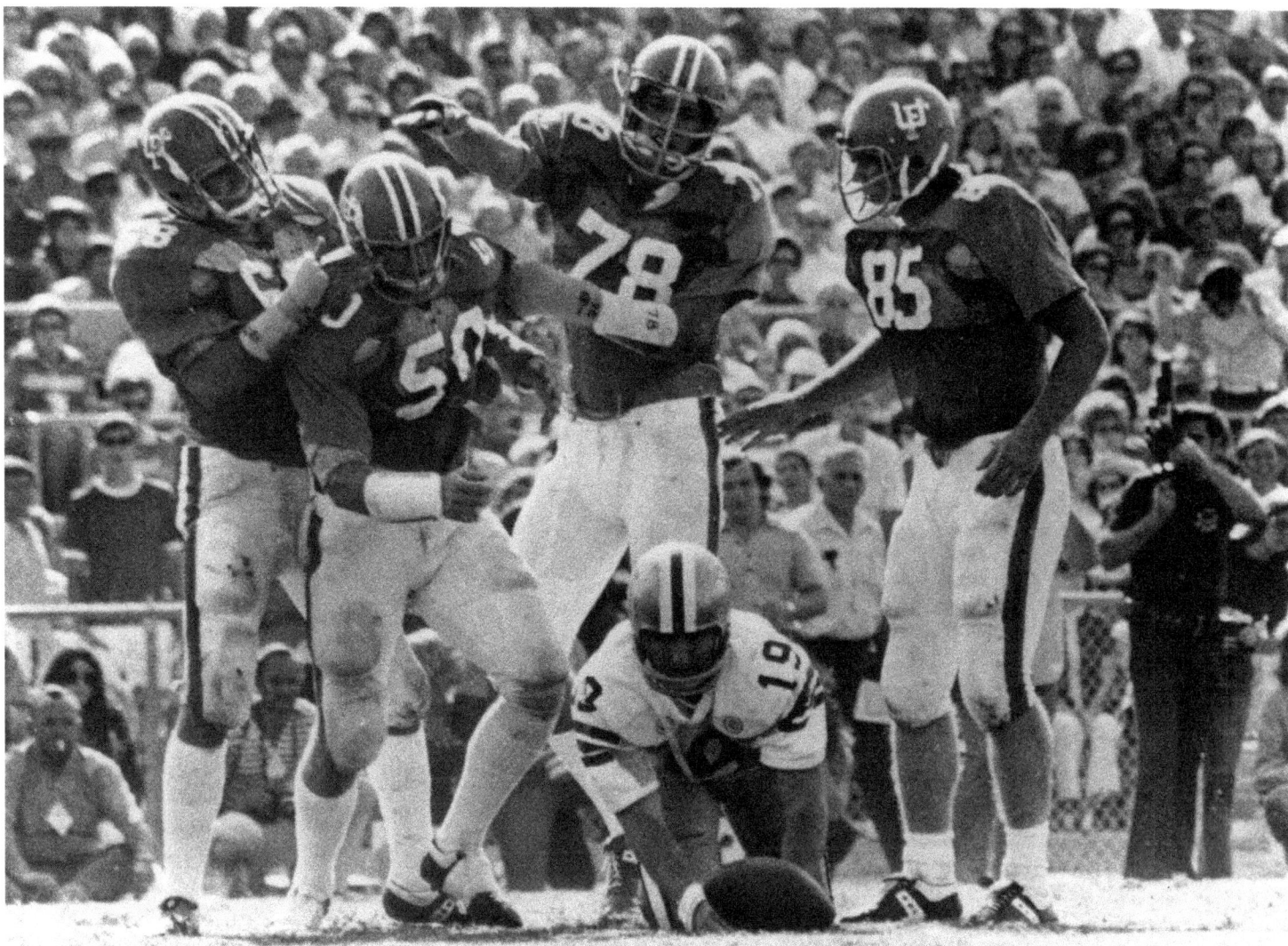

Gator senior and team captain Fred Abbott (no. 68) joined Ricky Browne (no. 50), Clint Griffin (no. 78), and Mike Moore (no. 85) in harassing opposing quarterbacks during the 1972 season, in this case FSU quarterback Gary Huff (no. 19). The thrashing they did to FSU that year, 42–13, was one of the largest margins of victory in the UF-FSU series. In fact, Florida's first 35 points were the result of FSU fumbles and miscues.

The first African-American to start at quarterback for the Gators was Don Gaffney, who played at UF for three years (1973–1975). His first start was against Auburn at Cliff Hare Stadium, where the Gators won for the first time ever. In November of that year, Gaffney led his team to victories over Georgia, Kentucky, Miami, and FSU, followed by a trip to the Tangerine Bowl.

Coach Ray Graves, who stepped down as head coach of the Gators in 1970 to become UF's athletic director, brought a care and benevolence to his players that they responded to with reciprocity. His players from the foregoing decade bonded so closely that they have continued to meet annually for a "Silver Sixties" reunion.

Four players who made up the 1977 Gator backfield were (left to right) quarterback Terry LeCount, fullback Earl Carr, halfback Tony Green, and halfback Willie Wilder. LeCount, Carr, and Green went on to play in the National Football League. Tony Green was the SEC Freshman of the Year (for 1974) after he broke Nat Moore's single-season rushing record with 856 yards on 133 carries.

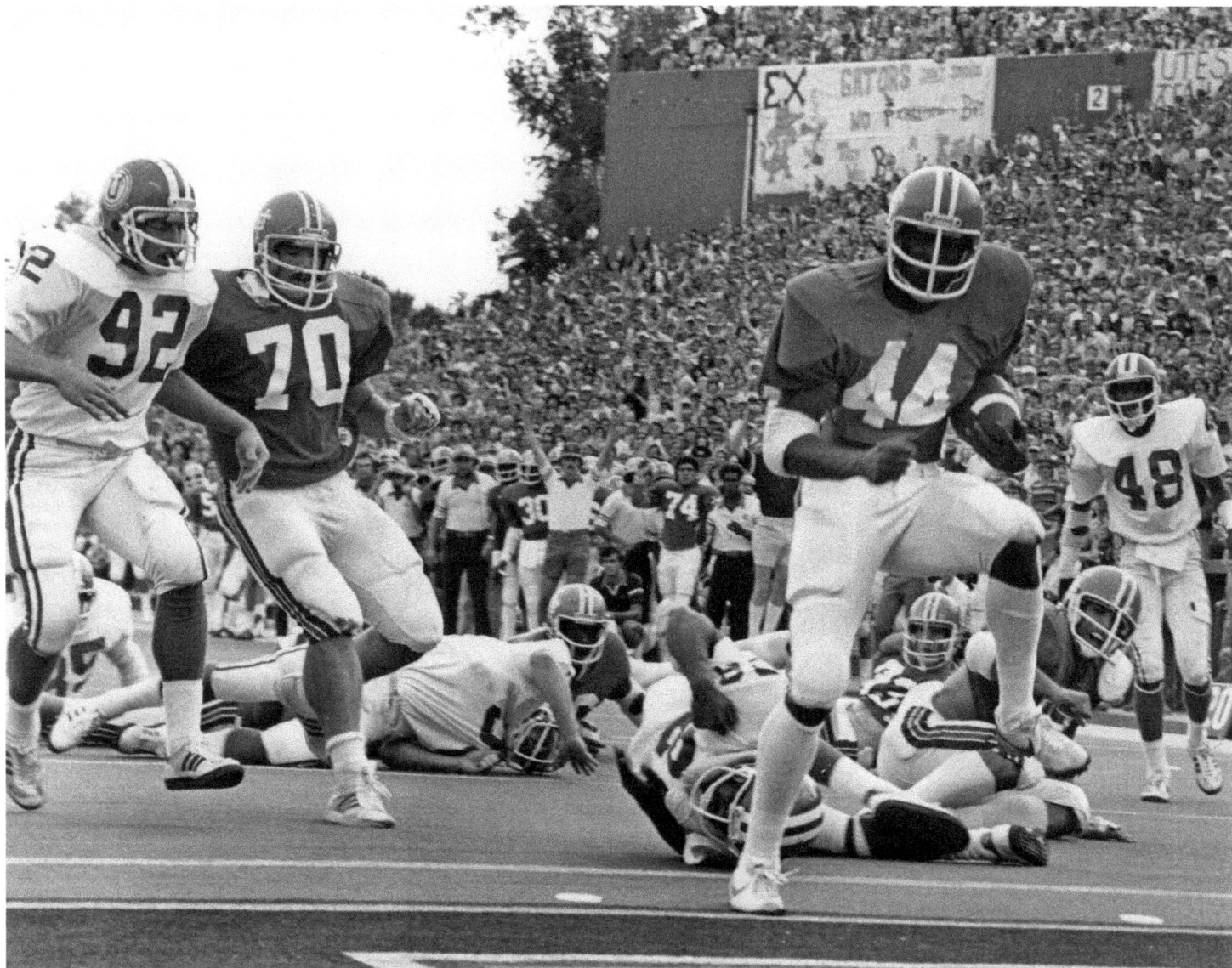

Dennis Forrester (no. 70), seen here at left blocking for halfback Willie Wilder (no. 44) in 1978, and his twin brother, David Forrester, both of whom lettered for three years (1975–1977), anchored a strong offensive line. There would be other twin brothers who played for the Gators over the years.

Coach Ray Graves (at left) escorted New York Yankees' owner George Steinbrenner onto Florida Field in 1978. Steinbrenner was a strong supporter of Gator athletics, including football and baseball, and helped fund improvements to the athletic facilities.

Yancey Sutton lettered for the Gators in football (1978–1980) while playing for two UF coaches: Doug Dickey and Charley Pell. He refused to let his deafness hold him back and went on to become a professional golfer after college.

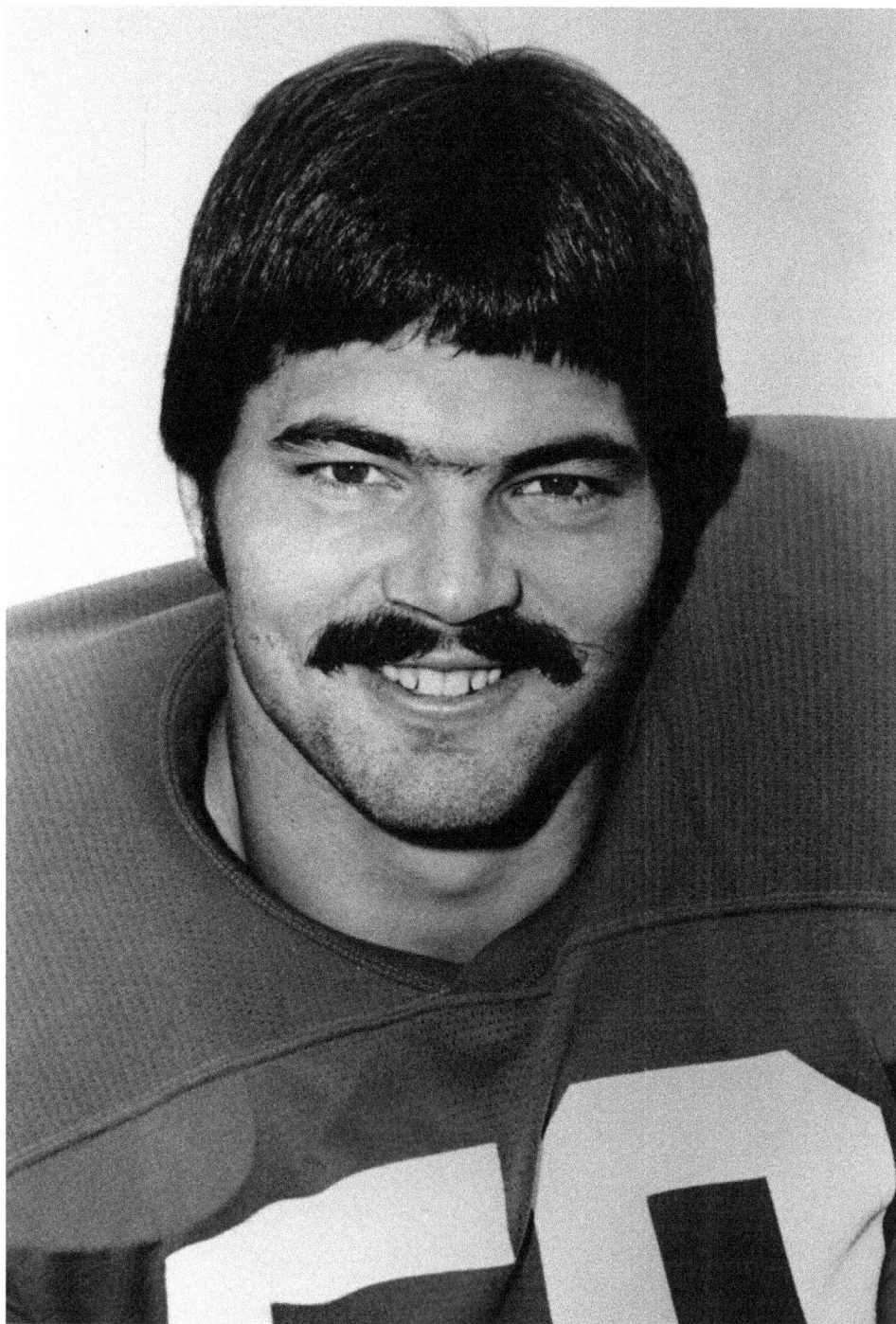

Dwayne Dixon (no. 83) lettered at UF (1980–1983) before going on to play in the NFL (1984–1985, 1987) and the Arena Football League (1987–1991), where he had the unusual distinction of twice winning the prestigious "Iron Man" award for his skills. He also coached UF's wide receivers in the 1990s.

Doug Dickey, who had grown up in Gainesville and played quarterback for the Gators (1952–1953), became the team's 15th head coach in 1970. He held the post for nine years (1970–1978), compiling a 58-43-2 record before becoming the athletic director at the University of Tennessee. He was inducted into the National Football Foundation Hall of Fame in 2004.

The 1978 team photo shows the quarterback coach, Steve Spurrier (top row, third from right) in his first coaching position. He would go on to coach at Georgia Tech (1979), Duke (1980–1982), for the Tampa Bay Bandits (1983–1985), and at Duke again (1987–1989) before returning to his alma mater as head coach in 1990. He excelled at each school, as he would do at UF.

In an ongoing evolution of the gator mascot, this particular one featured a rather mild reptile costume. The problem was that temperatures inside the outfit could surpass one hundred degrees. The mascot, which does not talk and therefore has to mime a lot, would later become Albert the Alligator and be joined by Alberta.

Alabama head coach Paul "Bear" Bryant (at left) and Gator head coach Doug Dickey were two of the leading SEC coaches in the 1970s. When Bryant retired from coaching in 1982, after 25 years leading the Crimson Tide, he held the record for most wins as a head coach at the college level. His recruitment of black players for his 1971 team helped lead to the integration of southern teams.

The large scoreboard at the north end zone was a far cry from the puny one at the south end zone, which stood from the 1930s to the 1960s. Florida Field's capacity had been increased to 62,800 in 1966 and would become even larger as the teams continued to excel. It would also be known as one of the noisiest stadia in the country.

In 1979, school officials had the Stephen C. O'Connell Center for basketball, nicknamed the O'Dome, built near the football stadium. Both would see their teams win national championships in the decade of the 1990s and would be the scene of graduations, concerts, political rallies, and Gator Growl, the student-run extravaganza held the night before the homecoming game. The first-rate facilities for football and basketball helped recruit star athletes.

"Passing up" a fan in the stands became a favorite activity on the student side of the stadium in the 1970s. The students sat on the north side, facing the sun, so they usually wore comfortable, even skimpy clothes, unlike fans in the past, when alumni and students alike dressed up for the weekly games.

In 1979, UF hired its 16th head coach, Charley Pell, whose record after five and a half seasons (1979–1984) was 33-26-3. After a bad first year (0-10-1), the Gators won eight games in 1980 for the biggest turnaround in NCAA history up to that time. Fan support enabled the school to increase the capacity of Florida Field to 72,000 in 1982.

Linebacker Scot Brantley from South Carolina lettered at UF for four years (1976–1979) and was later named to UF's Team of the Century. An injury ended his Gator career, but after UF he played professional football for the Tampa Bay Buccaneers (1980–1987) and in the 1990s became a broadcaster for Gator games. He has also had a daily radio show out of Tampa.

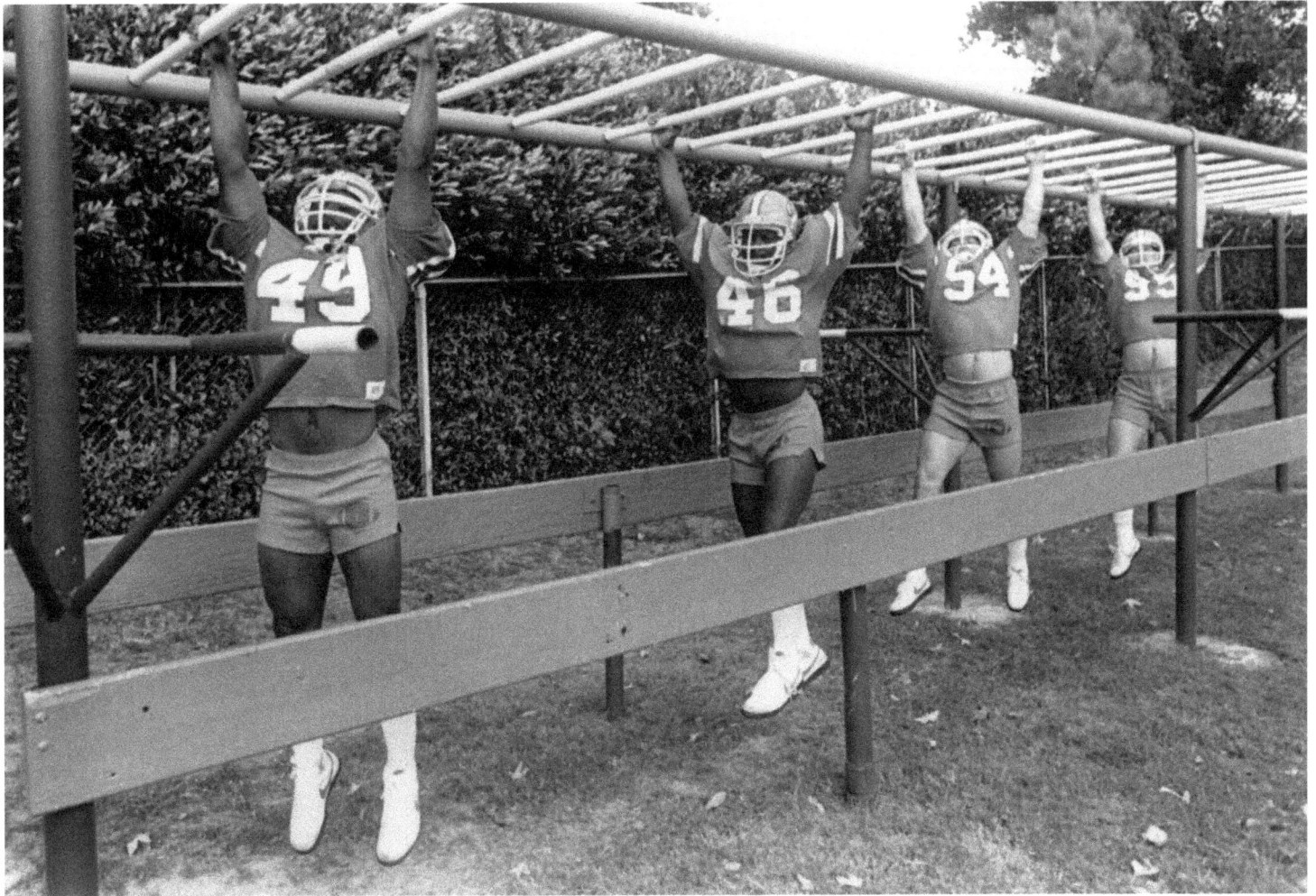

Coaches like Charley Pell stressed conditioning of the players, hired strength coaches, and conditioned the team to the difficulty of playing in the heat and humidity of Florida Field. When the Gators lost to bigger teams like Nebraska, the coaches recruited larger players who could hold their own on the line. Coaches Spurrier and Meyer also stressed speed among the receivers.

Wide receiver Cris Collinsworth lettered at UF for four years (1977–1980). While playing quarterback as a freshman, he tied the NCAA record for the longest touchdown pass, a 99-yard toss to Derrick Gaffney in 1977. He was a first-team All American (in 1980) before playing in the NFL for the Bengals (1981–1988) and then becoming a TV announcer.

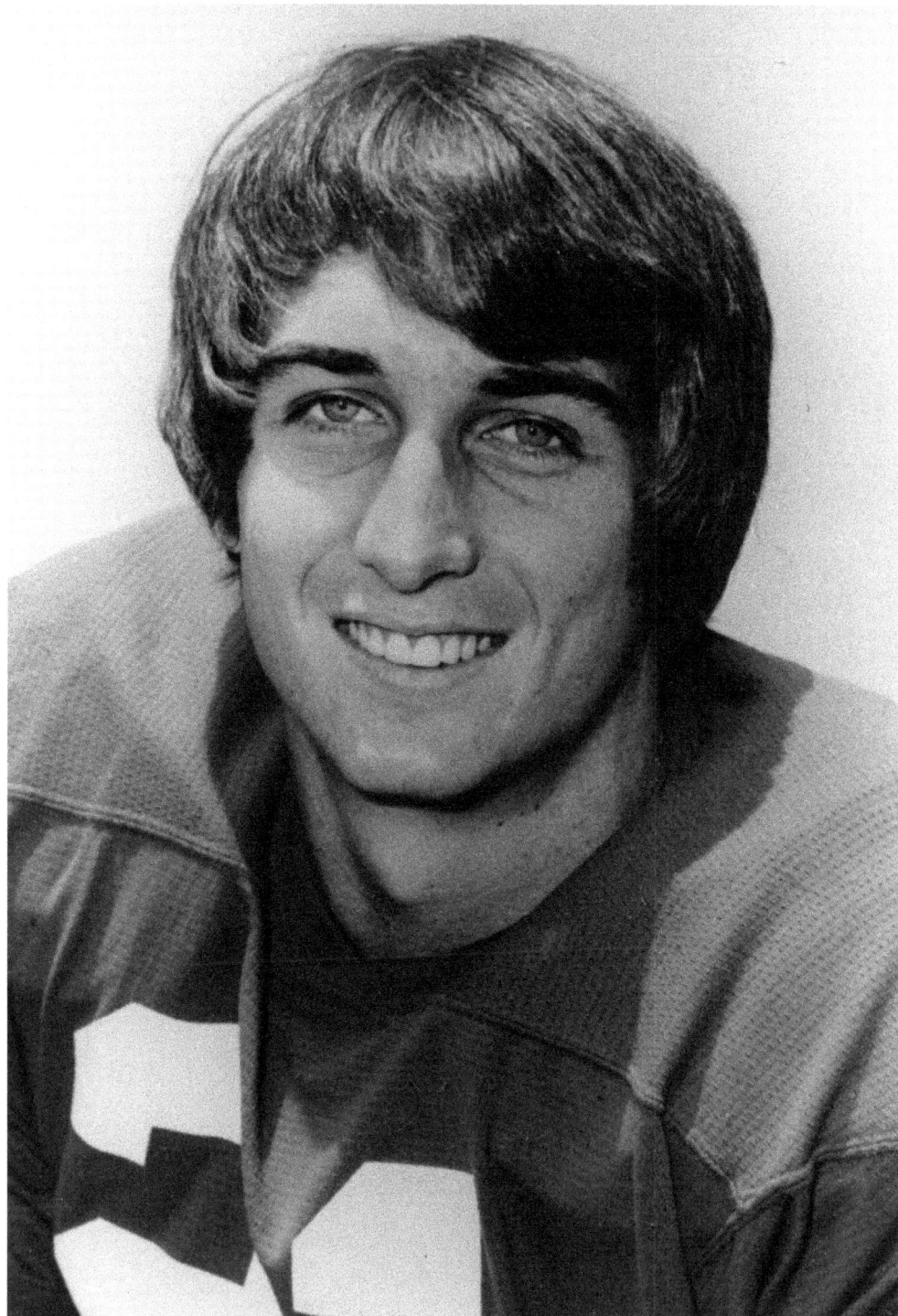

The 1980 Gator win over Maryland in the Tangerine Bowl, 35–20, ended a remarkable 8-4 season after the disastrous 0-10-1 1979 season.

One of the most effective Gator quarterbacks of the 1980s was Wayne Peace (no. 15), whose 1982 70.3 percent completion rate broke the NCAA single-season record. He and the other UF quarterback, Bob Hewko, led the team to an 8-4 record that year, achieved with strong runners like Neal Anderson, James Jones, and John L. Williams, as well as a strong defense with stars like Wilber Marshall.

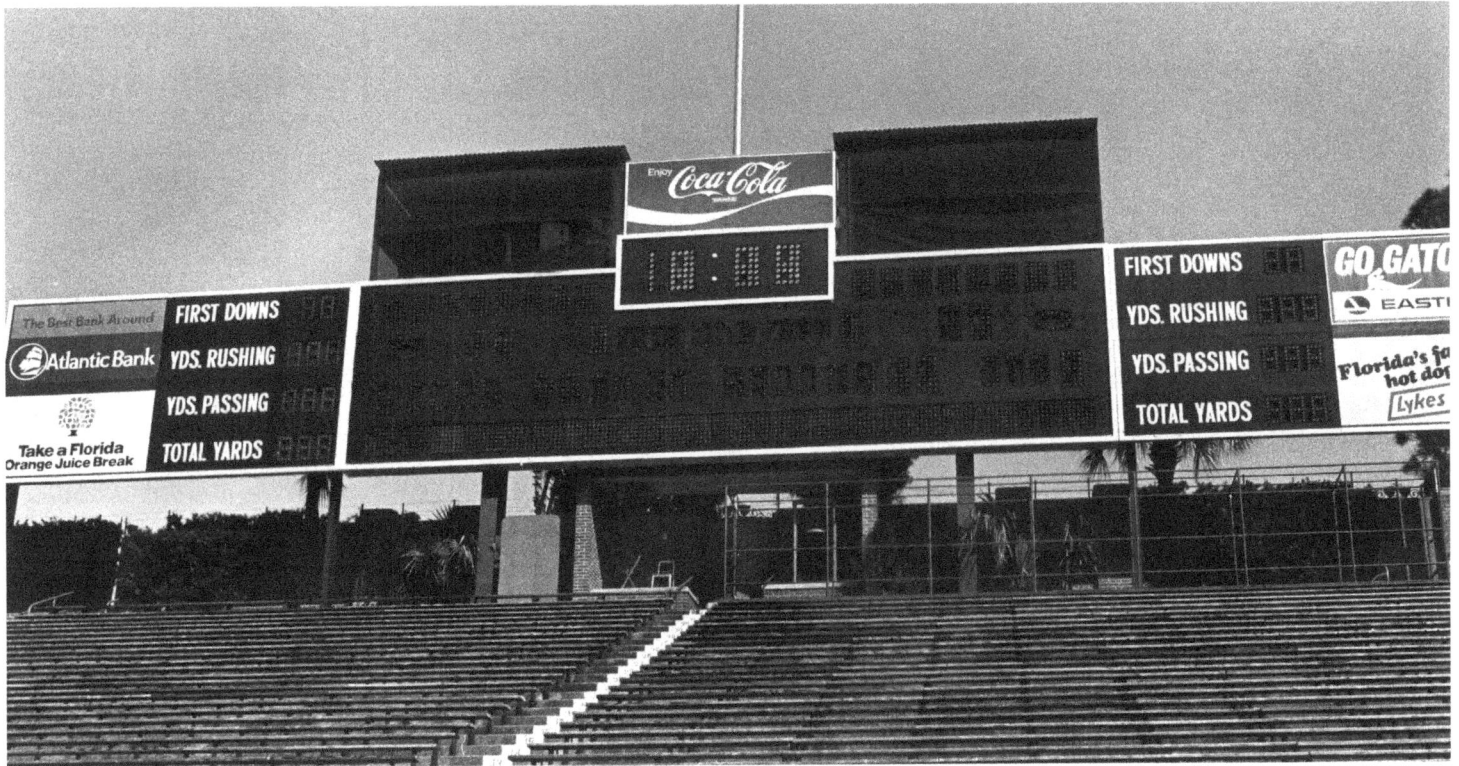

As more sponsors agreed to help with improvements to Florida Field, workers erected a larger scoreboard able to give fans more information about the status of a game.

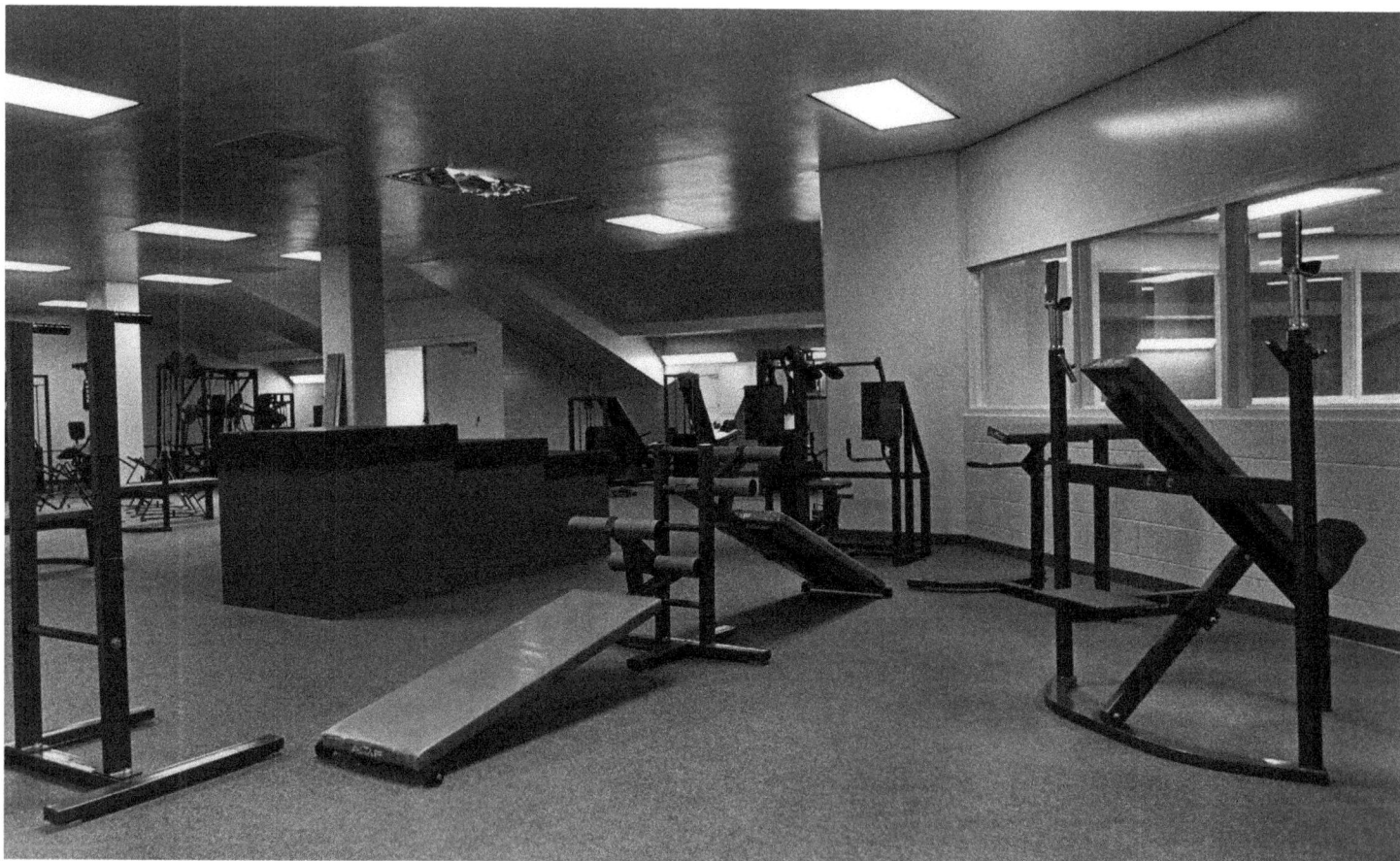

Football coaches had a new weight room built in their quest to build up the strength and stamina of the players.

Among the Gator players chosen to the 24-member SEC All-Academic team in the early 1980s for their scholastic success were (clockwise) kicker Brian Clark (no. 3), nose guard Robin Fisher (no. 66), wide receiver Spencer Jackson III (no. 89), wide receiver Broughton Lang (no. 2), quarterback Wayne Peace (no. 15), guard Dan Plonk (no. 65), and defensive back Vito McKeever (no. 36).

UF fans tore down the goalpost at Florida Field after the Gators defeated the Seminoles 35–3 behind the pinpoint passing of Wayne Peace, who completed 20 of 33 passes with four touchdowns. It was UF Coach Charley Pell's first victory in the UF-FSU series and one that he himself called his "greatest win."

Wilber Marshall (no. 88), seen here returning an interception, was named to the first-team All-SEC three consecutive years (1981–1983), All American (1982 and 1983), and nation's "Defensive Player of the Year" by ABC-TV (1983). The Chicago Bears picked him in the first round, and he played 12 seasons in the NFL for five different teams, becoming All-Pro three times (1986, 1987, 1992).

Albert (at left) and Alberta were photographed in 1983 standing in front of an alligator prop used in a movie. Other schools have used the alligator as a mascot, among them Allegheny College, Green River Community College, San Francisco State University, and San Jacinto College, but UF has become the school most closely associated with the reptile. Thousands of fans have done the Gator Chomp at Florida Field to intimidate foes.

At homecoming festivities on the night before the big football game, Gator Growl often featured big-name celebrities like Bob Hope, seen here with Melissa Burke, the 1983 Homecoming Queen. Over the years, off-color shows of some of the performers have embarrassed some alumni, but entertained many students.

Fullback John L. Williams (no. 22) threw a block for quarterback Wayne Peace (no. 15) in a 1983 game against the Seminoles. Williams was the first Gator player to rush for more than 2,000 yards and catch passes for more than 700 yards (1982–1985). The NFL Seattle Seahawks drafted him in the first round (1986). Williams played for them (1986–1993) and for the Pittsburgh Steelers (1994–1995).

The 1983 defensive squad of the Gators that held foes to an average of just 13 points a game included, from left to right, Tony Lilly (no. 18), Randy Clark (no. 81), Mark Korff (no. 59), Bruce Vaughan (no. 47), Alonzo Johnson (no. 93), and Wilber Marshall (no. 88). Lilly, Clark, Johnson, and Marshall later played in the NFL. Although the offense often snagged the headlines, the defense did much to win games.

Head Coach Charley Pell races out onto Florida Field between offensive star Lorenzo Hampton (no. 7) and defensive star Wilber Marshall (no. 88) in 1983. Tailback Hampton the next year caught a 54-yard touchdown pass from Kerwin Bell against Tulane to begin a string of eight consecutive wins that year.

One assistant coach at Florida in the 1980s who went on to the NFL was Mike Shanahan, offensive coordinator for four years (1980–1983). During that stretch, the Gators went to four bowl games, two of which they won. He became the head coach of the Los Angeles Raiders (1988–1989) and later the Denver Broncos (1995–2008), where he won back-to-back Super Bowls (1998, 1999).

As a freshman quarterback at Florida (1984), Kerwin Bell had a passing efficiency that ranked first in NCAA history for a freshman. Bell, a walk-on quarterback from Mayo, Florida, started for the Gators for four years (1984–1987). In that time he became the SEC's all-time leader in touchdown passes (56) and passing yardage (7,581). He later played in the Canadian Football League and became a coach in Florida.

Lorenzo Hampton (no. 7) was one of the effective Gator runners in the 1980s. As a four-year letterman (1981–1984), he rushed for nearly 2,000 yards. After UF, he was a first-round draft choice, playing for the Dolphins in the NFL (1985–1989).

Galen Hall took over from Charley Pell as head coach in 1984 and had a very good record of 40-18-1 in his five-plus seasons (1984–1989). His 1985 team was the first Gator team to be number one in the nation during the season. He was fired in the middle of the 1989 season and replaced by defensive coordinator Gary Darnell.

The 1984 Gator cheerleaders had a lot to cheer for: a new coach (Galen Hall), one of the best Gator quarterbacks (Kerwin Bell) and runners (John L. Williams), a great string of consecutive wins (eight), and a strong finish in the SEC (first). Offensive tackle Lomas Brown made the first-team All-America squad in his fourth year as a starter for UF.

UF president Marshall Criser and Head Coach Galen Hall, who replaced Charley Pell in 1984, hold the New York Times National Championship Trophy and the 1984 SEC Championship Trophy that the team had won. The SEC took away the SEC Trophy in 1985 because of NCAA infractions. Galen Hall had a 40-18-1 record in his five and a half seasons (1984–1989).

In 1985, because the UF football program was on NCAA probation for violations during the Charley Pell era, the players and fans considered the annual game with rival FSU their "bowl" game. After the Gators had beaten the Seminoles, 38–14, for the fifth straight time, the players, including senior running back Neal Anderson, came out onto the field to thank the fans for their support.

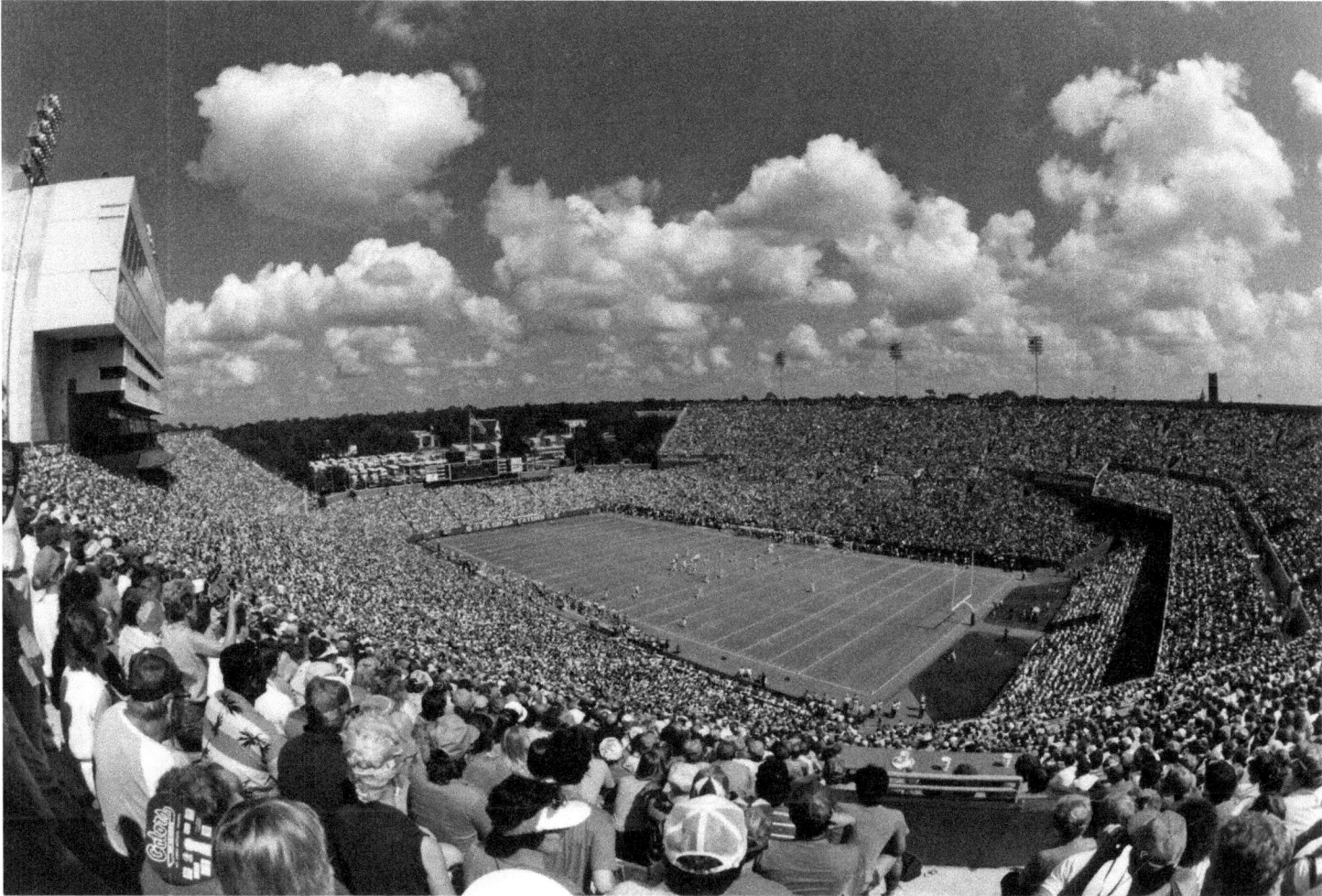

As the team began to win consistently in the 1980s and 1990s, Florida Field sold out week after week. The newly built skyboxes brought in much revenue to the Athletic Association, as did the fees paid by major television studios wanting to broadcast the Gator games. The field was also used for the annual high school state championship game.

After a win, the Gators have celebrated before the media, in this case after a game in 1985 against FSU. More recently the athletes from both teams have gathered at midfield to say a prayer of thanks, especially if there were no serious injuries during the game. In the Urban Meyer era, the Gator players went to the student section to sing the alma mater with other students.

Because athletes like Kerwin Bell are often greatly admired by youngsters, UF encourages its athletes to make presentations at schools and local meetings, where they can urge students to do well in academics, refrain from using drugs, and become model citizens. They often stress the fact that very few high school and college athletes compete at the professional level and that therefore the students are behooved to do well in school.

Emmitt Smith (no. 22) lettered at UF for three years (1987–1989). In 1988 he set school records for rushing yardage in one season (1,599), carries (284), rushing touchdowns (14), and rushing yards in one game (316 against New Mexico). After setting 58 school records, he left for the NFL after his junior year and starred for the Dallas Cowboys (1990–2002).

The coeds at UF who were part of the Twirlers or Dazzlers, as seen here in 1988, entertained the fans during halftime in the Swamp. They spent long hours practicing and traveling to away-games and were effective in rallying Gator fans in victories and in defeats.

Students who pass between the library and Peabody Hall on the modern campus will notice the statue of President Albert Murphree, one of the early presidents of UF (1909–1927) and a strong supporter of athletics. Murphree once said, "I consider football the most important sport in which a college student can engage."

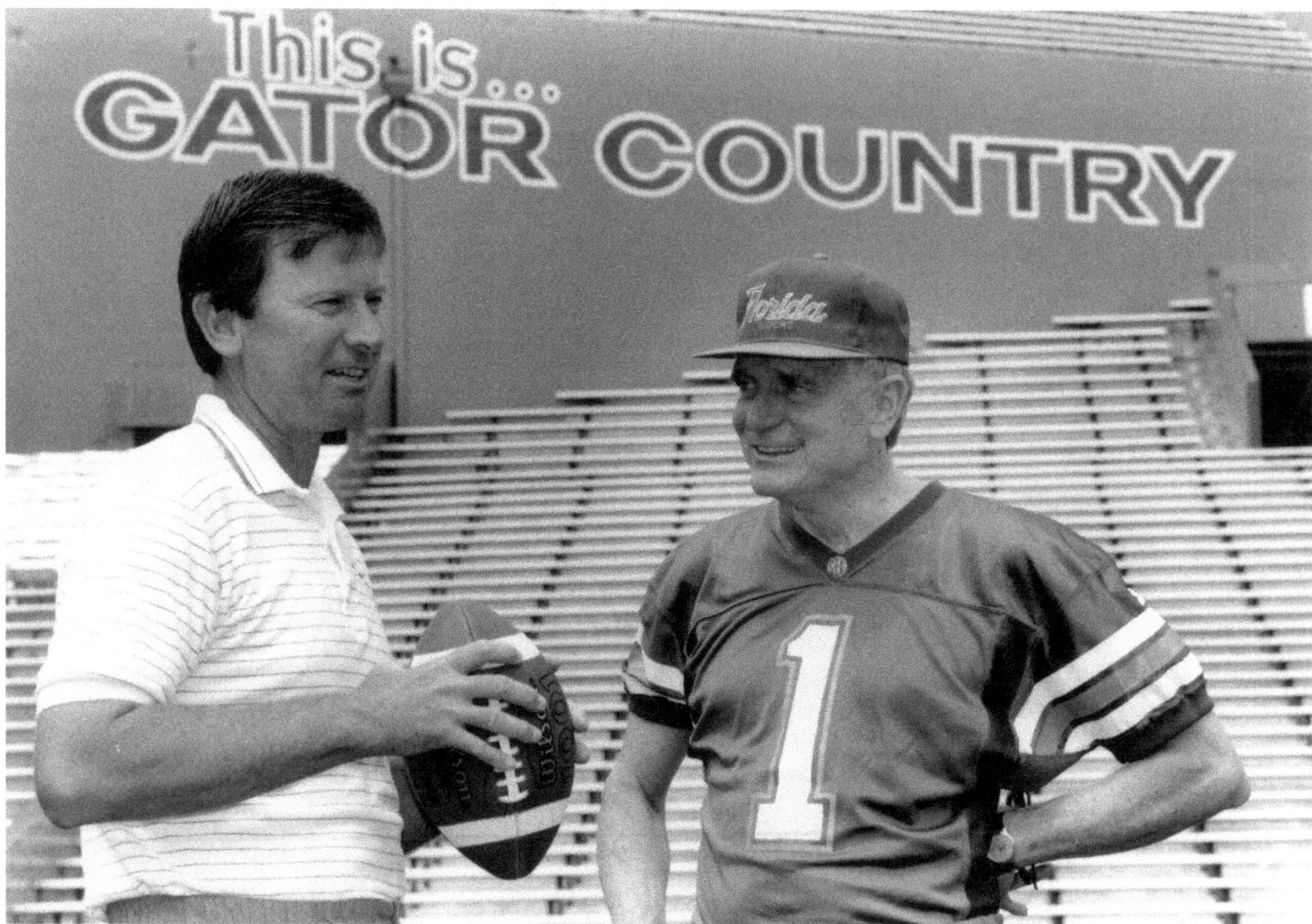

Steve Spurrier, UF's first Heisman Trophy winner (1966), became the school's 19th head coach in 1990 and compiled an outstanding record of 102-21-1 in his time there (1990–2001). He had UF's second Heisman Trophy winner (Danny Wuerffel) and the school's first national championship team (1996). This photo shows him with the popular Florida governor Lawton Chiles. Spurrier has more recently coached in the NFL and at South Carolina.

Shane Matthews, who began the 1990 spring practice fifth on the depth chart, worked his way up to the starting position and was a first-team All-SEC quarterback every season he started at UF (1990–1992). The tall, lanky thrower was a natural in Steve Spurrier's high-octane offense, and he ended up being named the SEC Player of the Year (for 1990). He went on to play in the NFL until 2007.

Former Gator and Chicago Bears running back, Neal Anderson, returned to Florida Field in 1990 with his father, Tommy, to display a plaque commemorating their establishment of a women's tennis scholarship in honor of Neal's mother, Dorothy. Athletes like Neal Anderson have generously supported the university, where they did so well.

Coach Spurrier brought many talents to the coaching ranks, including an enthusiasm that infected the players and crowd, innovations in a fun-'n'-gun offense, the determination to make Florida Field alien gridiron for opponents, and a desire instilled in many high school athletes to join him for exciting football. His insistence that workers replace the synthetic playing field with real grass probably helped mitigate many injuries to his players.

For more than 50 years George Edmondson, Jr., of Tampa, Florida, has been known as Mr. Two Bits for leading the fans in a "two bits" cheer from the middle of Florida Field. As shown here, he has also given scholarships to cheerleaders, some of the unsung heroes of Gator games.

An important academic issue for all college sports has been the graduation rate of athletes. Because the better athletes have sometimes left college for professional sports before they graduate, academic advisors do their best to encourage the athletes to earn degrees, even after leaving school. Here President John Lombardi congratulates football player Carlton Miles at the latter's graduation in 1992.

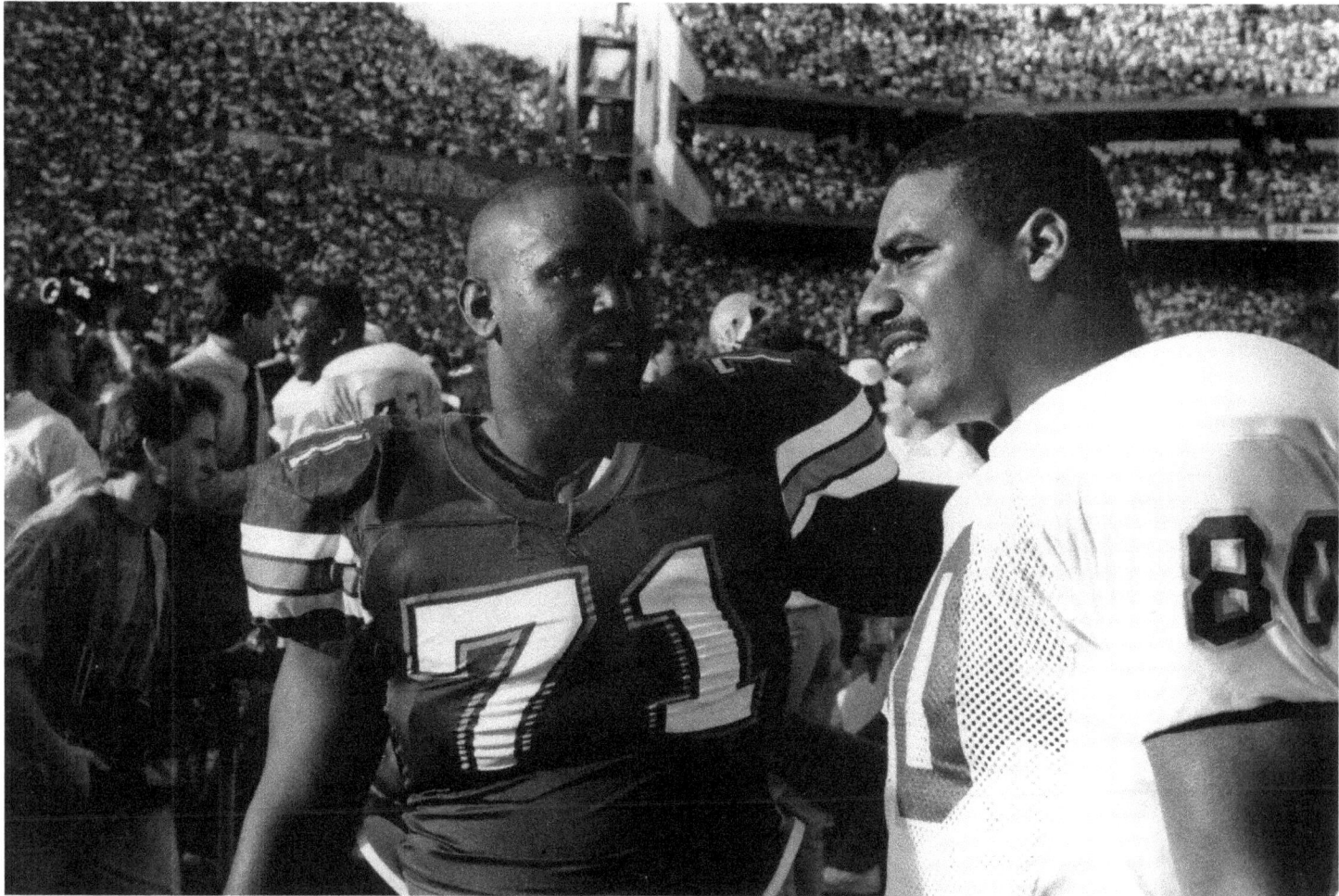

Often after a game, especially against an intrastate rival like Miami or FSU, players from each team, especially former high school teammates, meet in the middle of the field to reminisce. Fierce high school rivals have often become teammates at the college level, or high school teammates become college rivals, something that also happens at the professional level. Here Gator Tony McCoy (no. 71) talks with Seminole Johnny Clower in 1991.

Coach Spurrier poses with his coaches and players from the 1993 SEC champion team during an outstanding 11-2 season. He is flanked by runner Errict Rhett (no. 33) and linebacker Ed Robinson (no. 41). The win over Alabama in December was UF's first win in the SEC championship game and a prelude to its win over West Virginia in the Sugar Bowl.

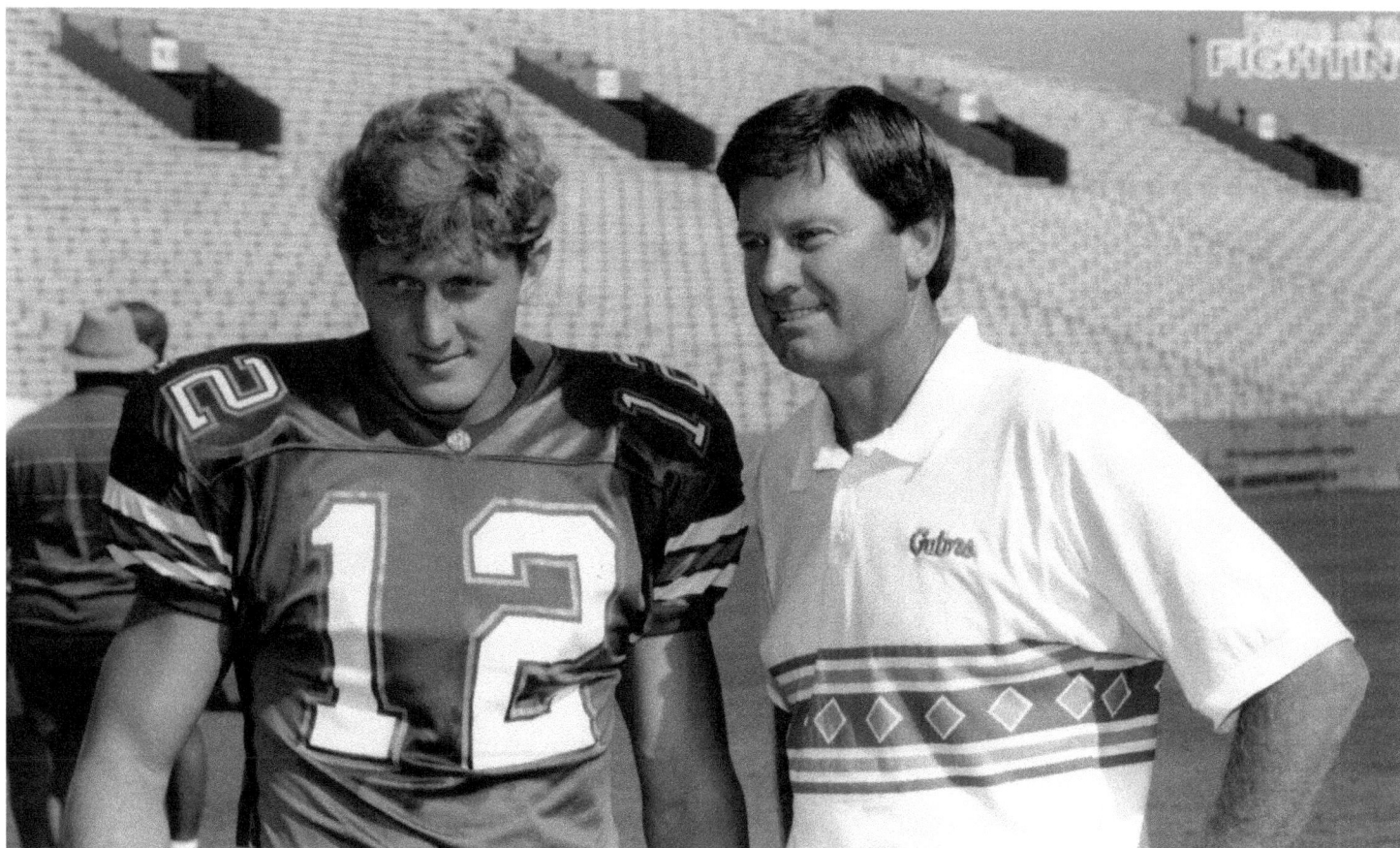

One of the many quarterbacks that Coach Spurrier made into better players was Terry Dean, who lettered for four years (1991–1994). He was on Gator teams that became the first in school history to win 10 games in one season and win an outright SEC title (1991), the first to win 11 games in one season (1993), and a team that beat the Georgia Bulldogs for a record fifth straight year (1994).

In 1996, the year the Gators won their first national championship, Danny Wuerffel won the school's second Heisman Trophy. That year he had a pass-efficiency rating that was first in NCAA history. He led all quarterbacks in the nation in touchdown passes in 1995 (35) and again in 1996 (39). After UF he played for several NFL teams before retiring in 2002 to work on charitable projects in New Orleans.

The national championship and other accomplishments would be repeated in 2006 and 2008 with the national championship won by Coach Urban Meyer's Gators. In both 1996 and 2006, the Gators won the championship despite having the toughest schedule, according to NCAA statistics. In 2007, quarterback Tim Tebow became the first sophomore to win the Heisman Trophy.

Athletic Director Jeremy Foley (at right) is shown presenting a check to Director of the Libraries Dale Canelas as Provost Andrew Sorenson (at left) looks on. The Athletic Association has used some of the money generated in the frequent appearances of the football team in post-season bowl games for the university library and for helping to fund the building of the Academic Advising Building, which serves all the students.

The football stadium has grown over the years—from initial construction in 1930 to periodic seating additions to a $17 million expansion in 1990 to the building of more skyboxes and press facilities in the 2000s. The glass bell-jar entrance pictured here, the Touchdown Terrace, and the curving ramps leading to new seats on the north end have helped make Florida Field one of the premier stadia in the country.

Notes on the Photographs

These notes, listed by page number, attempt to include all aspects known of the photographs. Each of the photographs is identified by the page number, photograph's title or description, photographer and collection, archive, and call or box number when applicable. Although every attempt was made to collect all data, in some cases complete data may have been unavailable due to the age and condition of some of the photographs and records. The photographs in the Archives at the University of Florida are identified as "UF Archives" without an identifying number because they are grouped by subject or time period. Photographs from specific collections in the UF Archives include the name of the collection.

II **1942 Athletic Fields**
UF Archives

VI **1911 Faculty**
Florida State Archives
Rc21229

X **1906 Sign**
Florida State Archives
Rc21225

2 **1884 Sketch of Gainesville**
Florida State Archives
Rc03553

3 **1900 Florida Agricultural College**
Florida State Archives
Rc04953

4 **1902 Team EFS**
Florida State Archives
N044027

5 **1902 Florida Agricultural College Team**
Florida State Archives
RC06300

6 **1905 Sketch of UF Campus**
Florida State Archives
Rc12045

7 **1907 Team**
UF Archives

8 **Roy Corbett**
UF Archives

9 **1908 Team**
UF Archives

10 **1908 Game**
UF Archives
uapc 1155

11 **1909 Team**
UF Archives
postcards 627

12 **1910 Team**
Florida State Archives
PR13085

13 **1912 Team with President**
1913 UF yearbook
no page no.

14 **1912 Floyd Hall**
Florida State Archives
Rc07092

15 **1915 Team**
1916 UF yearbook, p. 94

16 **Scene at Football Game**
1917 UF yearbook, p. 104

17 **1922 Champions of the South**
1923 UF yearbook, p. 106

18 **1922 White House Visit**
UF Archives

19 **1923 Team**
UF Archives

20 **Early Gator Home Game**
UF Archives

21 **The Team That Fought the Army**
1924 UF yearbook, p. 104

22 **Robert "Ark" Newton**
1924 UF yearbook, p. 105

23 **Ed Jones**
1925 UF yearbook, p. 124

24 **Baby Gators**
UF Archives

25 **1926 Hawkins Trophy**
1927 UF yearbook, p. 122

26 **University Auditorium**
Florida State Archives
N044226

HISTORIC PHOTOS OF UNIVERSITY OF FLORIDA FOOTBALL

When the Florida Agricultural College in Lake City became the University of Florida and moved south to Gainesville in 1906, it had a very fledgling football team, although worthy opponents were difficult to find. Little by little, as the school increased in size and reputation, its football team attracted higher-performing athletes and sterner opponents until it was willing to play any team in the country.

In 1966, the team had its first Heisman Trophy winner, but it was not until 30 years later that UF won its first national championship. Since then UF has chalked up two more Heisman Trophy winners and two more national championships.

Historic Photos of University of Florida Football chronicles the rise of one of the premier football programs in the country through hundreds of black-and-white photographs, each of them captioned and with introductions. The book includes photos of the university and the surrounding community to which the "Fightin' Gators" have become so much an integral part.

Kevin McCarthy has written 43 books, mostly about the history and culture of Florida, but also about Saudi Arabia, Ireland, and English grammar. He has a bachelor's degree from LaSalle College in Philadelphia and two degrees from the University of North Carolina, Chapel Hill: an M.A. in English and a Ph.D. in Linguistics.

He taught in Turkey in the Peace Corps for two years, in Lebanon for one year, in Saudi Arabia for two years, and at the University of Florida for 33 years. He has also given workshops on writing in Vietnam twice and lectured during more than 30 cruises.

WWW.TURNERPUBLISHING.COM